BORN *in* GOD'S LOVE

With Prayer
Martin
phil. 4/4

MARTIN E. IVES

BORN *in* GOD'S LOVE

MARTIN E. IVES

REDEMPTION PRESS

Published by Redemption Press, PO Box 427, Enumclaw, WA 98022
Toll-Free (844) 2REDEEM (273-3336)

Redemption Press is honored to present this title in partnership with the author. The views expressed or implied in this work are those of the author. Redemption Press provides our imprint seal representing design excellence, creative content and high quality production.

Unless otherwise noted, all Scriptures are taken from The Holy Bible, New International Version®, NIV® Copyright ©1973, 1978, 1984, 2011 by Biblica, Inc.® Used by permission. All rights reserved worldwide.

ISBN 13: 978-1-68314-763-3 (Print)
         978-1-68314-764-0 (ePub)
         978-1-68314-765-7 (Mobi)
Library of Congress Catalog Card Number: LCCN 2019908560

"Me?"

"Yes, you."

"Me!"

DEDICATION

To each one who wonders
what God has already recorded
on the answering service.

The Record

GATES AND BOUNDARIES

*W*HEN APPROACHING A GOD, we hope there will be open gates or invitations, and we expect there to be boundaries or limitations of knowledge.

Can a person of any culture have communication with God? The title *god* is used to indicate a being far more complex and superior to a human so that, of course, we humans cannot comprehend. Communication would seem to be a paradoxical suggestion—unless, unless such a god chooses to reveal its character and intentions.

How can one unique message possibly be applicable within any and every culture? There are already so many religions in the world, and each one has one or more gods. Often, too, different religions suppose that there is only one god. On what basis should one choose a god that is, hopefully, far superior to all the others? There is so much evil in our societies that many people question the value of any god.

Since there are other books claiming to reveal a god, does one need to read considerably to form a conclusion? The *Book*, the word used in this book for the Bible, means a record or account that claims to be a reputable source or record of God's presentation of self and the nature of humanity. Pages and pages record specific events along with the purpose of revealing this information. Quite surprising is the offer that the Spirit of God would affect the reader.

There are often times when I would *like* to know something, but admittedly, I don't always *need* to know. That may be a boundary, a limitation. One will often need to evaluate the importance of a question in relation to the main thesis. Some questions become trivial. A reader needs patience to allow an author to answer a question that may not be answered until many pages later. So be content to know that you will not understand everything about God. Understood? Understood!

I want you to note one specific offer recorded in the Book that opens a gate—an invitation: "Come near to God and he will come near to you" (James 4:8). How? Begin to accept that God is attentive to you as an individual. God may answer "Yes" to some requests and "No" to others. God loves you!

Two matters are declared to be inherent in every one of us of any culture:

1. "[God] has also set eternity in the human heart";
2. "Yet no one can fathom what God has done from beginning to end" (Eccl. 3:11).

The evidence of such is obvious, for all religions seek some future that is different from the now. Such a future includes a trepidation that after bodily death comes a meeting with God. Yes, indeed, as the Book says, "Face judgment" (Heb. 9:27). Job confessed, "What will I do when God confronts me? What will I answer when called to account?" (Job 31:14).

Yes, there are matters I do need to know. God promised long ago to help us know what we need. "Things revealed belong to us and to our children forever" (Deut. 29:29). Responsibility is ours to follow. It seems God anticipated our queries. "But these are written that you may believe that Jesus is the Messiah, the Son of God, and that by believing you may have life in his name" (John 20:31). This is a premise we should trust.

Here is another boundary: We cannot trust our own emotions, but must seek answers outside ourselves. "The heart is deceitful above all things and beyond cure" (Jer. 17:9). After reading many pages of the Book, we observe that it is a piece of literature, history, three intermingled biographies (God, people, and Satan), and a multitude of revelations of God's character and interventions on behalf of people.

Speaking of Satan, it would be good to have an introduction about him. Satan is prominent in the first pages of the Book, but then he is not conspicuous for many pages. "But woe to the earth and the sea, because the devil has gone down to you! He is filled with fury, because he knows that his time is short" (Rev. 12:12). In the opening pages with Adam and Eve, Satan did not exhibit fury, but showed politeness and authority. We will learn that his helpers are called evil spirits or demons.

As a result of guidance and after reading a thousand pages, we see that God's opinion is that people do not have an excuse for not knowing God's plan for them. For example, Jesus said, "If I had not come and spoken to them, they would not be guilty of sin; but now they have no excuse for their sin" (John 15:22). More evidence will be provided.

Within the first part of the Book, you will learn that you have been born in God's love! "Know therefore that the Lord your God is God; he is the faithful God, keeping his covenant of love to a thousand generations of those who love him and keep his commandments" (Deut. 7:9). You can ignore God's love, but you cannot extinguish it! The grievous reality is that if you choose not to be bothered with God, your desire will be fulfilled at a time in the future when you will be ushered out of God's presence forever—irreversibly.

Your challenge in reading the Book as a book is to let go of ecclesiastical words from your training and to start with the meaning of the words the skillful translators (translating mostly from Hebrew and Greek) have given us in our mother tongue. If you can read the newspaper, you can read the Book.

If you have existing attitudes that demean the Book, then read it as a novel while asking God to guide your attitude.

During past centuries, the neglect of the Book has brought tears to God's eyes, as expressed by the words *not listen*, recorded by Jeremiah at least a dozen times. That seems to be the same today where a Holy Bible sits on a shelf gathering dust. Intentionally, Jesus appeals, "I stand at the door and knock" (Revelation 3:20). The tour de force goal is: "See what great love the Father has lavished on us, that we should be called children of God" (1 John 3:1).

Yes—the Book is a history (His-story) revealing God. God's communication recorded in the Book will be found to be clear in any language, both spoken and written! With such offers and boundaries, let's go together through the Book and invite the Spirit of God along. The Spirit of God might change your life!

Choosing God's love as the theme, let's skim through the Book and learn what God's love includes.

GENESIS 1–6

FROM GENESIS CHAPTERS 1–6

*G*OD WILLED. THE SPIRIT OF GOD HOVERED. An immense creation took place over several periods of time. We have learned that the "stuff" that was created is very immense and complex. God was pleased.

The record that "There was evening, and there was morning" (chapter 1) is unique. It seems to indicate that when one phase stopped, there assuredly would be a next phase. The fifth day also has that expression that there would be a next event! Animals *and* people!

For now we will leave alone the complexity of God as "Spirit" and the use of "us" and "we," and will attend to the glorious events immediately ahead.

God willed this next event to be significant in a very different manner from the "stuff." God created Adam out of the earth. God very personally breathed life into him (Gen. 2:7). That first appears to be the same as for animals, yet later in the Book we will see that people will be included in a future opportunity for eternal life with God! God gave animals instinct. People were given free will.

In the meantime, here on earth we are made in God's likeness. Physically? Obviously not. Included in God's likeness is the ability to have mutual communication of thoughts and words—between the grand disparity of

Creator and this specially created one. Presumably, God was in some visual form. That was a mutual love relationship! People were *born in God's love*!

As we come to reflect, we see that all the "stuff" of the earlier creations is not as much loved as people, nor can there be a response to God's love from these other created things. God loves us—people. *Does that include me?*

The Lord God formed Adam out of the earth and placed him in an ideal and abundant setting called Eden (the Hebrew word means "delight"). The Lord God commanded Adam to enjoy eating fruit of all the trees except from one tree called the Tree of the Knowledge of Good and Evil. "And the Lord God commanded the man, 'You are free to eat from any tree in the garden; but you must not eat from the tree of the knowledge of good and evil, for when you eat from it you will certainly die'" (Gen. 2:16–17).

The Lord God paraded the animals before Adam, suggesting he name them. Adam did so without a command, apparently out of love. If this were a test, then Adam passed.

While watching animals as male and female, Adam realized he was without a companion. The Lord God made Eve from Adam's body! Adam responded exuberantly. Both Adam and Eve were physically naked, yet were apparently comfortable.

A third personality (Satan) abruptly appeared, likely in some visual form (at least non-frightening), and singled out Eve. He contradicted God and proposed an element of pride if they would eat the forbidden fruit.

We need to "cheat" by reading from the back of the Book. "But woe to the earth and the sea, because the devil has gone down to you! He is filled with fury because he knows that his time is short" (Rev. 12:12). That's the nature of Satan. However, with Adam and Eve, he concealed that personality and appeared thoughtful and authoritative.

Pause here to think of two words: *test* and *temptation*. A test is a presentation of at least two options ahead. The premise is that the teacher, in this case God, has already given enough evidence for the student to understand the outcome of each option, especially the one the teacher wishes for the recipient. The teacher wants the student to pass, not fail. A temptation is a presentation (here the temptation is by Satan) in which the presenter wants the choice to be the opposite of the teacher's. The choice would not be made by instinct, but by free will.

Remember that Adam had been told not to eat the fruit from one specific tree, or he would die. However, just looking at the fruit was appealing. Society would have said to Adam, "It's a no-brainer." Some people would have said, "Watch out! Pride is apt to override intelligence." It did.

They ate that one fruit!

What happened?

Adam and Eve spurned God's love and sovereignty!

How?

They changed their view of the godhead! In their inner beings they chose to change from having God as ruler to placing self as god! In plain English, "I will decide without the need of reference outside myself." The incontrovertible evidence was their behavior of eating that fruit. They had spurned God's love!

Next comes a little dramatic supposition. God approached Adam and Eve with a knife in hand and with a sheep accompanying him. They tried to chat about what God had said. Both trembled. Suddenly God killed the animal and washed the fur.

God placed the skin (fur) of an animal on Adam and Eve. Apparently that was different from physical comfort. It was a tit-for-tat life substitution! It was also a symbol of God's continued sovereign presence.

Adam and Eve did not die. They lived! Did they jump up and down for joy and shout, "We live!"? Did they bow in silence with tears running down their cheeks? Neither is recorded. How sad, not even thanking God.

Their recorded reaction was fear and hiding. Realizing they had thrown off God's sovereignty, they sensed their nakedness. Here is an illustration: I have been driving a car for decades, usually by myself. Twice recently with a friend, I realized I was in the passenger seat, and I burst out saying, "I feel naked." I was without sovereign control of the car.

Adam blamed Eve, and Eve blamed the serpent. That is currently called "the blame game." Our society today does that well, extending that one step further by suing the person who is blamed.

We need to pay attention to our Bible translators, who were careful. In the first chapter we are given the title *God*, one word. There was no personal relationship with the created "stuff"—the non-loving. The translators next used the words *Lord God* because, obviously, the Hebrew word changed. *Lord God* is used in relationship with people. We will observe throughout the Book that *Lord* is a distinctive title for a person who has authority over a given group of people to say, "You live" or "You die." Applying lordship, God could choose either to let live or let die apart from any court proceedings. The Lord let them live!

God had said that if they ate of the fruit of that one tree, they would die. Let's use the word *separation* to illustrate "die." God put Adam and Eve out of Eden, separating them from his immediate presence (whatever that appearance had been). When our bodies die, we are separated from this earth-life, and the body and soul are separated. The body returns to the dust. For the soul, think of the coach of a sports team removing a player from the game and assigning him to the bench; the player continues to exist, although temporarily apart. Later in the Book we find that the apostle Paul names that existence *asleep*. "But Christ has indeed been raised from the dead [from among those separated from this earth-life and having the soul continue to exist], the firstfruits of those who have fallen asleep" (1 Cor. 15:20). Thus, God had Adam and Eve only die in the sense of separation from his personal presence rather than from earth. Note that Jesus rising from the dead (from among the existing separated ones) is distinctly different from saying he was raised from death.

The Lord God put Adam and Eve out of Eden—decidedly so. They could not return to eat of the Tree of Life. Spurned love demands separation. Upon divorce, there is separation. Upon civil disobedience, there is separation from society. But remember the fur. Adam and Eve were separated from God's immediate face-to-face presence—a mild form of dying—but they continued with assurance of God's sovereign presence! We will watch for the use of *voice, visions,* and *dreams.* "Let live" was also assurance that God had a future plan. Part of it was that female and male would have considerable difficulty living. God acted quickly, not allowing time for reform of behavior nor considering the best results of two-out-of-three tests. Knowing Adam's heart, God apparently knew that the result would be the same.

The one offended has the right to design a restoration, and God began that with the presentation of the fur. There is no hint in the record of Adam and Eve asking for restoration. Sad.

Back to the sequence. God used the life of an animal as a substitute for the life of Adam and Eve. The animal had no behavioral problems. It was the inner essence of life that needed replacement. God's love continued in a different setting. Exodus 15:13 refers to it as "unfailing love"! This is reinforced by a statement a little later in the Book: "Know therefore that the Lord your God is God; he is the faithful God, keeping his covenant of love to a thousand generations of those who love him and keep his commandments" (Deut. 7:9). God's love continues even for us today, despite how inconsistent we are.

Serious consequences become more apparent with Cain and Abel, the sons of Adam and Eve. During a worship time (maybe they were teenagers), Cain offered produce of the soil and Abel offered a firstborn of his flock. The Lord reprimanded Cain, for he knew better. He had learned from his parents about offering the life of an animal that God had made. Abel had followed God. Both Cain and Abel used free will. Cain allowed his emotions to control him, and he killed Abel. (The "bad guy" killed the "good guy," as so often happens today.) Why all this? The conclusion is simple—the change of the inner being to self-as-god was hereditary in Cain and Abel, and it continues in us today! Abel rose above his self-interest to please God. The self-as-god appeared during the next centuries with the appraisal given that "every inclination of the thoughts of the human heart was only evil all the time" (Gen. 6:5). The critique was of the inner being and was evidenced by the outward behavior. A list of behaviors need not be given.

Notice the spiritual help provided during the time of Adam and Eve to Noah. First, the help was by Adam and Eve, who lived nine hundred years and had some three hundred thousand evenings to share with kin around a bonfire, munching sheep burgers with "s'mores" (honey on flatbread). Surely they repeated how God had so graciously treated their mistake and how he had offered one life one time only in place of their lives. Note that God, not Adam, put forth the substitution animal. How many kin listened?

Second, Enoch had nearly one hundred thousand days to warn people. "See, the Lord is coming with thousands upon thousands of his holy ones to judge everyone, and to convict all of them of all the ungodly acts they have committed" (Jude 14–15).

Third, Noah had thousands of opportunities to speak. Basically, Adam and Eve, Enoch, and Noah were repeating oral history (not oral tradition). The lives of all three well covered the two thousand (a round number) years to the flood. How many people of those generations trusted the substitute that God provided? We don't know. Those who did believe died and were separated from earth-life along with the others. How long you live on earth is not important compared to being ready for "restoration" (resurrection) in the future.

The Lord God was grieved (using a human term) and announced a shortening of the life span (slowly) (Gen. 6:3). God announced to Noah that he would destroy the people. God told Noah to build an ark. He gave directions that would protect Noah's family and many animals. Noah obeyed, and they were protected.

An observer exclaims, "Hooray! This is the kind of God to seek. God wills and loves! Events are in accord with God's plan of love."

Some scientists put before us evidence of humanlike creatures who lived ages before Adam and Eve. One suggestion is simply that they were a different creature. God placed a new, very different creature, in the persons of Adam and Eve. Notice the evidences already given of how unique they were. Thank God that you and I are of this "breed." In a similar vein, readers often heatedly enter arguments as to how long (ages or twenty-four-hour days) were the creation periods. Both sides can give Scripture references that seem to pertain. The short response is to shake hands, sit down, and return attention to the main subject. Both sides should say, "I'd like to know, but I don't need to know!" Neither one needs to move and start a new church.

One curiosity is who wrote all of this, especially the part at the beginning when no people were present. We hope an answer will be given in the next few pages.

There is value in the word *separation*. Our society thinks of the body dying as annihilation, ceasing to exist. Separation carries along, in a subtle way, the thought, the wish, that there might be a restoration in the future. God gave Adam and Eve the assurance that love continues, and *then* he applied the partial separation. The Book will present confidence of a resurrection by Christ Jesus and of entering his presence!

God let the evidence of the inherited self-as-god nature blossom for about two thousand years. Apparently there was not much thankfulness or worship of God to record. Maybe a few people responded to Adam and Eve, Enoch, or Noah. The behavior throughout was the crime sheet of evidence of evil from their inner beings that continued to spurn God's love!

What was the guide for life in those years? One relationship—love. Life on earth continued under the presence of God's love given to all people. The life of one animal was a loving substitute for all people who would accept/believe God's continuing loving presence. Any examples? Enoch and Noah "walked with God." How? By talking to God, giving thanks, praising/worshiping God. Sadly, Adam and Eve are not so listed. A lifestyle of love can be used under any civil rule and in any society, even today! "Against such things there is no law" (Gal. 5:23). God cannot change.

Here is one more illustration: The husband at the end of the meal feeds the dog and then proceeds to dry the dishes. (This, before the time of dishwashers, shows the author's age.) He does so out of love without a command or request. There were no commands (directives) for living during these first two thousand years! Love precedes commands and does not need commands!

God pronounced that "death" upon Satan sometime in his future would be by a human offspring of Eve! The question arises, How can an offspring of Eve (Adam is not listed!) be superhuman enough to overpower Satan? Again, we need to be patient and continue reading the Book, hoping to find answers. How and when will the animal God used (beneath human dignity) be replaced? Can one "human" assist the billions of people we have now?

The Book is "biased," but not in the sense of being demeaning. Its subject material is very selective. The flip side is that we are thankful for material left out so that the Book is as small as it is.

One caution looms: People trained in churchy vocabulary will have difficulty. They will tend to place concepts into all this when they are not defined there. Several words frequently used later were not used during this two-thousand-year period. *Atonement* does not occur; *command* (only to Adam and then Noah); *hope*—zero; *King/kingdom*—zero; *sacrifice*—zero.

A multitude of evidence has been given to demonstrate God's love, which is also for you and me!

Confessing from one's heart the need for a perfect substitute and accepting God's constant love is a personal choice. Hence, that does not require an attachment to any religious group, no matter where one lives on this earth.

All of the above is missed when one skips these pages and begins reading in the Book with Abraham. These first few chapters form a prologue for the entire Book! God has given us the beginning of what we *need* to know. The Book is God's answering service. The Book reveals God and the character of people. May you learn to learn by reading the whole Book.

Having now read the first pages of the Book thus far, may we honor the Spirit of God and claim entitlement to read the rest of the Book. We carry forward convictions that (1) God loves all people—that is why he made them; (2) God has a grand reason for letting us live; (3) some "human" will overcome Satan; and (4) some "human" will be the final substitute for all people. If you do not believe this good news, why are you here in this earth-life?

As we continue through the Book, we will observe how consistent and persistent God's love is.

"Who am I? I am one *born in God's love*!" Never, never cease thanking God for that love. I am born with a self-as-god nature. Never, never cease thanking God for loving you as you are. Never, never cease thanking God for wanting you in his close personal presence in the future. God will never, never overlook one's confession of needing a perfect substitute. We don't need to know the details now, for we have assurance that God will adequately reveal his entire plan.

A reader asks God,

> "Me, loved by you, God?"
> "Yes, you."
> "Me!"

ADAM AND EVE'S TESTIMONY

*A*DAM AND EVE LIVED for over three hundred thousand days. Suppose they regularly had an evening bonfire serving sheep burgers and s'mores (honey on flat bread) for their kin. What might they have said to alert their loved ones about their lessons learned? Here are some possibilities:

We quickly saw that God talked with us rather than with the animals, which were moving about by instinct. We realized that God loved us apart from all the rest of the created "stuff."

We had no parents. God is our Creator-Father. We should have thanked God for the honor of being the first people, for having been made in a love relationship, and for our bountiful setting.

We had difficulty grasping the consequences of using our free will, which is so different from instinct.

We should have confessed to God that by our inner self we decided to act independently from God's pleasure and command. Instead, we actually blamed God. We thought we shamed God, whereas we were really the ones shamed. We should have admitted that we deserved to be put out of God's personal presence because a secondary god, self-as-god, does not belong in the presence of God.

We should have used the address "Lord God" to remind us of his authority to declare, "You live," or "You die." The Lord God, in accordance with his clear command and out of love for us, took the life of an animal as a substitute in place of our lives. We wondered about the animal being beneath our dignity or worth.

We neglected to appreciate and thank the Lord God for assurance of his continuing sovereign presence with us by giving us the fur of the animal as a daily reminder of God's gift of continuing love. We had not even asked for a sense of a continued loving relationship. The Lord God was showing his love constantly before we ever acknowledged our desperate need.

We soon found that we were prone to live daily as though we were our own gods and could decide on our own what we should do, and as we watched Cain and Abel, we realized that our new inner nature was hereditary.

We should constantly be grieved that in spurning the Lord God we had acted on pride rather than intelligence.

As the years go by and we see animals and some people die (separated from this life on earth), we wonder if there is some kind of continued life. The Lord God has put an inkling of such in us.

Please watch with us as we learn of the difficulties promised to each woman and each man. We wonder how an offspring of Eve will be able to produce someone powerful enough to overcome Satan. Our dear ones, we tell you our history and encourage you to tell others that the Lord God's love is upon all people, even people of grievous conduct.

How sad that there is no record of such expressions! In contrast, Enoch and Noah are honored as walking with the Lord God. May none of us today point a finger at Adam and Eve without admitting that the other fingers point back at us.

GENESIS 6 TO DEUTERONOMY

FROM GENESIS CHAPTERS 6–50

NOAH BUILT THE ARK according to the directions God had given him. The Lord caused the animals to come to Noah as directed, by twos and sevens. God shut the door on Noah, his wife, his three sons, and their wives. Immense flooding killed all the people and animals that had the breath of life. At this point, scientists and Bible scholars argue as to the dimensions of the flood. Suffice it to say that all the people were killed. The Lord's critique of people was the reason for this, and it is clearly recorded twice: "Every inclination of the thoughts of the human heart was only evil all the time" (Gen. 6:5), and "Every inclination of the human heart is evil from childhood" (Gen. 8:21). Notice that God critiqued the heart, not the behavior. People spurned God instead of recognizing love and seeking it.

God created a new beginning of people with the same intention; they too were to be lovers of God. Would they be better lovers of God than those who had previously lived?

God covenanted that such a flood would never happen again. Upon the flood receding and Noah leaving the ark, Noah built an altar and sacrificed animals, which gave a pleasing aroma to God. He remembered the oral history (not oral tradition) from Adam and Eve. As with Adam and Eve, offering the life of an animal (life for life) demonstrated our confidence of God's unfailing love. God bid them to have families and instructed them that all food was available.

The rainbow was given as the sign of God's covenant of love: "Remember the everlasting covenant between God and all living creatures of every kind on the earth . . . the sign of the covenant I have established between me and all life on the earth" (Gen. 9:16–17). The statement "on earth" doubled is truly valid. Rainbows are seen everywhere on earth over all cultures! God loves all people! You were born into this love!

Soon after God gave the rainbow as a sign of his love, people started to build a city and a high tower. The purpose is recorded: "Make a name for ourselves" (Gen. 11:4). No honoring of God is recorded. How sad! The Lord scattered them "over the face of the whole earth" and divided their once-unified language (Gen. 11:4–9).

Several generations later, the Lord spoke to Abram (Abraham), saying, "Go from your country, your people and your father's household to the land I will show you" (Gen. 12:1). One particular man out of how many in the city? A TV program would have great glee presenting the harangue that Abraham surely received from his kin and tradespeople. People today would have insisted on using a search committee to choose a new leader. God knew the heart of Abraham, even though he had come out of a culture of idolatry. The Lord announced his plan that Abraham would become a great nation and all the earth would be blessed through him. Preposterous? Simply put, the Lord willed it. Later, at the assigned location of the promised land, the Lord announced that Abraham's kin would be as the dust of the earth and that the land he was on would be his. Abraham then built an altar. Abraham believed the Lord.

Abraham politely invited God's attention to the fact that he did not have a proper heir. God replied that Abraham would indeed have a proper son and again told him that his heirs would be as countless as the stars. Abraham believed without argument. Such trust in the Lord brought accreditation of righteousness! "Abram believed the Lord, and he credited it to him as righteousness" (Gen. 15:6). Note that God's observation was of Abraham's inner self, not of his behavior. The Lord also gave a rather discouraging promise that these people would be enslaved for four hundred years. Even so, they would be blessed as they escaped. Again—love!

A secondary heir, Ishmael ("God hears"), was born, who would also be great and become twelve nations. God loves even those who ignore him.

The Lord God appeared to Abraham and announced a new covenant of circumcision for every male. This was a covenant of relationship between Abraham and his descendants and God Almighty, with many benefits.

At Abraham and Sarah's advanced age, there had been a moment of laughter, a struggle to believe, when God announced they would have the true heir, Isaac, whose name means "he laughs." Imagine the testimony Isaac could give to tradespeople when they laughed at him, explaining to them that he had been born of such aged parents, just as was promised by God!

Lot had moved into or near Sodom. The record indicates that "the people of Sodom were wicked and were sinning greatly against the Lord" (Gen. 13:13). Two angels appearing as men warned of God's impending judgment. The only evaluation of conduct recorded is the prominence of male sex. Not even ten "righteous" were there, and the Lord proceeded to destroy both Sodom and Gomorrah. An angel rescued Lot and his family. There always remains a remnant when God brings disaster. Watch for this in the next pages.

Listen to this from God: "Abraham . . . take your son, your only son, whom you love—Isaac—and . . . sacrifice him" (Gen. 22:1–2). Abraham and Isaac journeyed—with Isaac carrying the wood. An observer might ponder, "They had three days to turn chicken and run home." However, Abraham was confident that God would provide a ram. An angel stopped them at the last dramatic moment, and they sacrificed a nearby ram that God had provided for them. Not even a human sacrifice would have restored full fellowship with God. Note the stress on "only son." Suspense!

Abraham sent his servant to kinfolk to select a wife for Isaac. He conducted the search by praying frequently, and God directed the servant to

Rebekah. Isaac and Rebekah married, and soon they had twins, Esau and Jacob, with the Lord announcing that the older would serve the younger. In a moment of selfishness, Esau gave his birthright (being the "first born") blessings to Jacob and later wept in regret. Jacob fled Esau's remorseful wrath. After years of honest toil and being deceived by Laban, Jacob took Rachel as his wife.

The Lord tested Rachel through barrenness but finally gave her a son, Joseph. Joseph received a dream that in some way he would be superior to his brothers. He then had another dream that he would become superior to his parents. No explanation was given at the time. That caused jealousy and anger! The brothers sold Joseph to become a slave in Egypt. The plot was unknown to their father, Jacob. (Jacob was renamed Israel, meaning "one who strives or prevails with God.") Joseph was honored and dishonored in Egypt. The Lord gave him success, and upon interpreting Pharaoh's dream of seven years of famine, Joseph was placed second in command in Egypt. The widespread famine brought Joseph's brothers seeking food. Joseph severely tested them. When Joseph decided to reveal himself, he bid them (all eleven of them) to come closer. The tour de force must have been Joseph showing himself as circumcised.[1] Then they feared for their lives—even more so later after Jacob died!

Joseph's full response to his brothers was, "Don't be afraid. Am I in the place of God? You intended to harm me, but God intended it for good to accomplish what is now being done, the saving of many lives" (Gen. 50:19–20). Joseph died at age 110. We wonder what emotions Joseph had during his tumultuous years. Are we patient when we wonder why God has allowed a particular matter? Do we question God's unfailing love?

FROM EXODUS

The Israelites became so numerous that they were resented and then reduced to slavery. A Levite husband and wife had a son, Moses, in adverse

---

1 Circumcision is not explicitly said. "Polite" words are used. After giving a verbal explanation, Joseph bid them come closer (Gen. 45:4), presumably to observe his body intimately—the ultimate evidence.

civil circumstances. Moses, in the midst of slavery and after murdering an Egyptian, fled to kinfolk. Forty years later, God spoke to him from a burning bush that was not consumed! How gracious of God to use a spectacular method of presenting a frightening commission. Moses would be the instrument for the release of the Israelites from Egypt! God told Moses to tell them, "I AM WHO I AM . . . I AM has sent me to you" (Ex. 3:14). God is to be known as the God of Abraham and of Isaac and of Jacob. God is anchored in history. Again, God knows our hearts, and he knew that the king would not agree unless God's might compelled him. When Moses hesitated, the Lord gave two small miracles for assurance, and he sent along brother Aaron as a spokesperson.

God told Moses to say to Pharaoh, "Israel is my firstborn son" (Ex. 4:22). In that culture, the firstborn son inherited the responsibility of representing the father. Here, God is the Father. Here in the midst of love for all cultures is the distinctive assigned to this new culture. Pharaoh retorted, "Who is the Lord, that I should obey him and let Israel go?" (Ex. 5:2). The Lord affirmed to the people: "I will free you from being slaves to them, and I will redeem you with an outstretched arm and with mighty acts of judgment" (Ex. 6:6). Again, this is evidence of God's love.

The verbal conflict escalated, and God sent plagues, demonstrating his power: water changed to blood; frogs, then gnats, then flies covered the land; a plague came upon livestock; boils came upon people and animals; widespread locusts; and a "felt" darkness. In those sentences, *know* occurs ten times. Know what? The Lord is sovereign! The Lord further hardened an already hardened heart. *Lord* is used throughout. Remember, a lord has authority to say, "You live" or "You die." That authority was exercised next, as the firstborn male of men and of cattle died during the night. The Lord spared the Hebrew people from several of those calamities. As declared, when the angel of death saw blood on their doorframes, he passed over. There was no death there. The Hebrew folk were to remember and celebrate yearly. They still do so today, celebrating Passover.

The Hebrews lived in Egypt for precisely 430 years, as had been fore-told long before to Abraham (Gen. 15:13).[2] God continued to love the Israelites. Contrast that with the lives of those who had spurned God.

The whole multitude of Israelites and animals were "thrust" out, and they received abundant gifts as they left. Next, God directed them to face the Red Sea! God protected them as Pharaoh's chariots pursued. God used a wind to push the water into a wall on each side of a wide area of dry ground! It is interesting to consider the logistics: How many people and animals crossed? How many hours did it take? How long was the stretch of dry ground? The whole series of the Lord's unified miraculous incidents was evidence of the glory to be accredited to God, as declared several times. A song of rejoicing ensued. The Book is a record of God's loving help, even during judgment!

Soon after crossing the Red Sea, grumbling began. The Lord provided meat (quail) in the evening and manna (with the flavor of honey) in the morning, along with instructions. The Lord bid Moses to strike a certain rock. Water out of a rock? Yes. Adequate. Some people did not follow instructions well, yet God guided their movement. Moses was human, and the Lord encouraged him.

> The Lord, with boldness and clarity, told Moses to say:
> You yourselves have seen what I did to Egypt, and how I carried you on eagles' wings and brought you to myself. Now if you obey me fully and keep my covenant, then out of all nations you will be my trea-sured possession. Although the whole earth is mine, you will be for me a kingdom of priests and a holy nation. (Ex. 19:4–6)

This was another distinctive for this culture. That's love! That was only the heading for a contract to follow. They soon had the Ten Commandments! God "signed" it. "Wherever I cause my name to be hon-

---

2 The four hundred years mentioned in Genesis 15:13 was apparently a round number, as Exodus 12:40–41 specifically tells us that it was 430 years.

ored, I will come to you and bless you" (Ex. 20:24). Generous love again. The Ten Commandments were elaborated in great detail for daily living as an angel guarded the people. How gracious! An observer calls out, "No. No. Surely not!" Yes, and while Moses was meeting with God on Mount Sinai, Aaron sinfully guided the people to make a golden calf to worship the gods who had brought them out of Egypt! False—gods did not thrust them out of Egypt. God did! Moses arrived and strongly interceded. Many worshippers of the calf were killed by sword. God sent a plague. God then relented and again promised them the land. God's love prevailed!

A special cloud and fire in the sky from God were over them for all to see and to guide them with confidence. When the people cried to Moses for water, Moses cried to God for leadership. God's goal was given: "You are to be my holy people" (Ex. 22:31). He gave them assurance: "See, I am sending an angel ahead of you to guard you along the way and to bring you to the place I have prepared" (Ex. 23:20). That's God's daily attentive love, and it also expects their obedience.

After his many conversations with the Lord, Moses "wrote down everything the Lord had said" (Ex. 24:4). Thank the Lord for honest recording that we can read millennia later. Moses read from the book of the covenant to all the people, which was likely what he had written that far.

The Israelites were to build a sanctuary tabernacle by God's directions so that the Lord could dwell among them (Ex. 25:8; 29:45)! The Spirit of God guided people.

We have a new word—*atonement* (Ex. 29:33–37). It first applied to the cover for the ark, but mostly it refers to the covering for our sin in our relationship with God. Play on the word *at-one-ment*, which will be explained later (Lev. 17:11).

It is sufficient for now to know that in the Exodus record, *Lord* occurs almost four hundred times, mostly of the Lord in a relationship with a person or persons.

The Lord clearly announced many directives for worship and daily living. The death penalty was prescribed more than a dozen times. Specific dimensions for the tabernacle were recorded. The Lord's cloud and fire continued with the people. Surely that was enough guidance and protection!

Again the Lord directed Moses to write—for forty days (Ex. 34:27–28)!

The many, many sacrifices cost the families a large portion of their profits from their herds. They were paying, yes, but that was never enough. God paid the first time, although the animal was temporary. We wait for God to give the final sacrifice to restore a perfect fellowship with a holy God! Having glanced ahead in the Book, we know that will be accomplished by Christ Jesus himself.

There has not been any further mention of Satan.

God has been so gracious in unmerited situations:

- Allowing Adam and Eve to live
- Allowing Cain to live
- Allowing all to live for two thousand years
- Blessing Ishmael

Day in and day out, the Lord showed his love by his consistency, warnings, attentiveness, provision, and protection. The Israelites, with the moniker of God's "firstborn son" (Ex. 4:22), had been alternately hot and cold in God's loving relationship. The only adequate "Son of God," we will learn later, is Christ Jesus. The firstborn son in that culture was to be the adequate representative of the father. Hence, the Israelites were to represent God. "Son of God" is not simply an honorary title, but an assignment of responsibility.

Can you testify, *God, today I trust your love hovering over me. I desire your whole plan of restoration of fellowship*?

FROM LEVITICUS

Leviticus is a recording of many directives for sacrificing animals. It also includes laws regarding sanitation and even one's menu. Again, animals had not sinned and had no inner being pretending to be a god. Each sacrificial specimen was without defect. All was temporary.

One offering was distinctive. The lead priest was to offer a bull for atonement for himself and his family. Then he was to present two goats. One was to be a sin offering for the people. The priest was to lay his hands on the head of the other goat, confess the sins of the Israelites, and let the goat go free into the desert, a solitary place, as a scapegoat (Lev. 16). Skipping into the New Testament for a moment, we see that Christ Jesus did both! He died with the approval ("hands on") of God as our substitute for our atonement, and then he rose to life and went into the desert as our scapegoat!

A summary of the system of animal sacrifices is specific: "The life of a creature is in the blood, and I have given it to you to make atonement for yourselves on the altar; it is the blood that makes atonement for one's life" (Lev. 17:11). Atonement! Oh, yes, that is precisely what God did for Adam and Eve! An animal life was a substitution for a human life. Still, an animal is beneath the dignity (worth) of a person. All these sacrificial acts must be temporary. However, the atonement aspect satisfied God. The result of the fellowship offering (the NIV uses the word *fellowship*; some other versions use the word *peace*) for the person and family was fellowship of the unholy person with the holy God! We will learn that the only adequate atonement is the person of Christ Jesus (Rom. 3:25; Heb. 2:17).

Don't become smug simply by following rules. The next chapter, Leviticus 18, sternly warns against the customs of Egypt and Canaan. Sexual misconduct must have been prevalent, as that is the only subject listed and detailed for being outside of God's example of the husband-wife relationship.

Several feasts are prescribed in Leviticus that help with humility and rejoicing with the intent to thank God and give God proper glory. The Passover was very humbling, again with substitution of animal life for human. The Israelites were to give glory and credit to God for bringing them out of Egypt.

The death penalty is detailed more than a dozen times in Leviticus.

"These are the commands the Lord gave Moses on Mount Sinai for the Israelites" (Lev. 27:34—the last sentence of Leviticus).

Prior to the flood, God expected the people to respond to him out of love without laws. Now with laws, God expected them to realize that a high price was needed. They grumbled about the loss of profits from their herds. The reality was that God provided his creatures. Even then there was no complete final restoration of fellowship. When will we have the final answer? Meanwhile, an omen of death lingers in the air.

FROM NUMBERS

This begins with a census of several age groupings. The use of genealogies was very important. A person's importance was indicated by the record. Since the people did not have middle names or ID cards, the record distinguished each person (e.g., one could distinguish between three different men named John). Also, age clusters were used to assign responsibilities.

This wording appears often: "The Lord spoke to Moses." Apparently that was without God appearing in some visual form. "He heard the voice speaking to him" (Num. 7:89). With Moses, God also spoke "face to face" (Num. 12:8).

Spies were sent ahead into Canaan and returned with a mixed report. The people rebelled at the thought of advancing. Moses interceded with a reminder: "The Lord is slow to anger, abounding in love and forgiving sin and rebellion" (Lev. 14:18). The Lord's response was forgiveness. Nevertheless, the adults would die in the desert. The Lord said, "[You have] disobeyed me and tested me ten times . . . How long will this wicked community grumble against me? . . . For forty years—one year for each of the forty days you explored the land—you will suffer for your sins and know what it is like to have me against you" (Num. 14:22–34).

Moses struck a rock instead of speaking to it as God had told him to do. The Lord quickly responded that Moses would not lead the people into the promised land because of his lack of trust (Num. 20:12). Sometimes God's judgment takes place close to the event, and sometimes it takes place much later. A harsh episode was when God told Moses to tell the judges to kill their people who had worshiped the Baal of Peor (Num. 25:4–5)!

"Moses did as the Lord commanded" was the basis of his leadership, as recorded two dozen times in Numbers. The logistics of moving a few million people, as well as animals, is staggering. We have noticed that vengeance is the Lord's (live or die), and his prerogative was sometimes executed through human leadership.

How many times has God's love been shown by his picking the Israelites up and guiding them onward?

FROM DEUTERONOMY

Let's consider the entire book of Deuteronomy an epilogue to the previous four books. An epilogue is a review, an emphasis, a using of additional words and illustrations and likely more specific applications of purpose. Besides the sentences, an author highlights a subject by word repetition. Note some examples of this. *Bless* (or a form of the word in all these cases, such as blessing, blessed, etc.) is used thirty-three times in the book of Deuteronomy. *Chose* is used thirty-one times. *Covenant* is found twenty-eight times. *Curse* is used twenty-three times. *Destroy* is written forty-seven times. *Detestable* is found eighteen times. *Law* is used twenty-three times. *Out of Egypt* can be found sixteen times. *Possession* (of land) is in Deuteronomy twelve times.

Remember that God told Moses to tell Pharaoh that these people were to act as God's firstborn son (Ex. 4:22). What will Moses highlight as the principal character trait of the Father and the primary responsibility of these people as firstborn son?

Moses spoke to all Israel in the desert near the Jordan at the end of the forty-year wandering: "Go in and take possession of the land that the Lord swore he would give to your fathers—to Abraham, Isaac, and Jacob—

and to their descendants after them" (Deut. 1:8). People from six or seven nations had been listed as living in that land.

Here is immense praise of God: "What other nation is so great as to have their gods near them the way the Lord our God is near us whenever we pray to him? And what other nation is so great as to have such righteous decrees and laws as this body of laws I am setting before you today?" (Deut. 4:7–8).

Moses recorded cautions and encouragement for daily living. He honestly included embarrassments. The laws given previously were reviewed.

"But if from there you seek the Lord your God, you will find him if you seek him with all your heart and with all your soul . . . For the Lord your God is a merciful God; he will not abandon or destroy you or forget the covenant" (Deut. 4:29–31), even with outstretched arm (repeated five times in Deuteronomy). Again, notice that the concern is about the quality of the inner being rather than visible behavior.

Remember the basic covenant of love:

> Has any god ever tried to take for himself one nation out of another nation by testings, by signs and wonders, by war, by a mighty hand and an outstretched arm, or by great and awesome deeds, like all the things the Lord your God did for you in Egypt before your very eyes? You were shown these things so that you might know that the Lord is God; besides him there is no other. From heaven he made you hear his voice to discipline you . . . Acknowledge and take to heart this day that the Lord is God in heaven above and on the earth below. There is no other. (Deut. 4:34–39)

How does one respond to such a God? The Ten Commandments are repeated next! The first cluster defines one's relationship to God. In the midst of that is, "[God] showing love to a thousand generations of those who love me and keep my commandments" (Deut. 5:10). Soon after that we read, "Love the Lord your God with all your heart and with all your soul and with all your strength" (Deut. 6:5) This is followed by page after page of guidance.

The Lord chose this new nation "to be his people, his treasured possession" (Deut. 7:6). In addition to this, God expressed his love for them: "Know therefore that the Lord your God is God; he is the faithful God, keeping his covenant of love to a thousand generations of those who love him and keep his commandments" (Deut. 7:9). Yes, that is love!

"If you ever forget the Lord your God and follow other gods and worship and bow down to them, I testify against you today that you will surely be destroyed" (Deut. 8:19). "On account of the wickedness of these nations, the Lord your God will drive them out before you" (Deut. 9:5). That was the condition for which God directed killing people. Back to Israel: "What does the Lord your God ask of you but to fear the Lord your God, to walk in obedience to him, to love him, to serve the Lord your God with all your heart and with all your soul?" (Deut. 10:12). How many times does that need to be said? God observes your heart attitude more than your behavior.

"See, I am setting before you today a blessing and a curse—the blessing if you obey the commands of the Lord your God that I am giving you today; the curse if you disobey . . . by following other gods" (Deut. 11:26–28). The ball was in their court. The response is one or the other, even for us today!

These first five books of the Book formed the Bible for the Hebrew people for years.

"The Lord your God will raise up for you a prophet like me from among you, from your fellow Israelites. You must listen to him" (Deut. 18:15). As we read the entire Book, we recognize that Christ Jesus is that Prophet (cf. Matt. 17:5; Mark 9:7; Luke 9:35).

Notice that the first fourteen verses of Deuteronomy 28 are specific blessings for obeying and pleasing God and are very brief. However, verses 15–68 spell out the results of not obeying God! That long list indicates that God knows us better than we think, or admit, we know ourselves. God is blunt and straightforward. All this has been the same God—the God of

Abraham, of Isaac, and of Jacob. How much clearer could Moses be? The attitude of "I will be safe, even though I persist in going my own way" will bring disaster (Deut. 29:19).

Be selfish for a moment. Read all of Deuteronomy and count the number of promises for the person who pleases God. Do you find more than two dozen?

There is no excuse. "The secret things belong to the Lord our God, but the things revealed belong to us and to our children forever, that we may follow all the words of this law" (Deut. 29:29). Again, we have no excuse!

God directed Joshua to be the next leader. Moses wrote again. What an honorary epithet was added as the last sentence of the book of Deuteronomy: "For no one has ever shown the mighty power or performed the awesome deeds that Moses did in the sight of all Israel" (Deut. 34:12). That is not simply honorary; it is a stark reminder of what Moses did and why!

Let's close with excerpts from chapter 30:

> And when you and your children return to the Lord your God and obey him with all your heart and with all your soul according to everything I command you today . . . The Lord your God will circumcise your hearts and the hearts of your descendants, so that you may love him with all your heart, and with all your soul, and live [be prosperous] . . . if you obey the Lord your God and keep his commands and decrees that are written in this Book of the Law and turn to the Lord your God with all your heart and with all your soul.
>
> Now what I am commanding you today is not too difficult for you or beyond your reach. It is not up in heaven, so that you have to ask, "Who will ascend into heaven to get it and proclaim it to us so we may obey it?" Nor is it beyond the sea, so that you have to ask, "Who will cross the sea to get it and proclaim it to us so we may obey it?" No, the word is very near you, it is in your mouth and in your heart so you

may obey it . . . Love . . . walk . . . keep . . . you will live and increase
. . . Now choose life . . . The Lord is your life.

The guidance given prior to the flood, the covenant of love (Deut. 7:9),
continues the same afterward.

Note from the above again the succinct record of the character of the
Lord as Father and the responsibility of the firstborn son (cf. Ex. 4:22)! Do
you believe?

We casually say that Moses recorded these matters, and we leave the
first impression for the public that he contrived the early events as if writing a novel. Instead, the events have been imbedded in human history.
Hence, the authority of what we read basically rests upon the character of
the people, and more than that, the character of God. The consistency of
the particulars authenticates the Book as a whole. Our ultimate confidence
in this Book is by means of the Spirit of God hovering over Moses and
others later. Therefore we say that the Bible is God-inspired; that is, the
Spirit has subtly been the editor in chief regarding what was included and
what was intentionally left out. The Book reveals God and exposes people.
Behold, the incomprehensible God is comprehensible. God has defined for
us a problem and assures us of a future solution.

Yes, Moses was the obedient recorder. On the other hand, he had no
possibility of knowing or even supposing that God wanted it preserved
and read years—even centuries—later, and he had no concept that these
five records would be assembled as one integrated authority of the nature
of God and of people and that it would become guidance for any culture
of the world!

Even for us, the pages of these five books present the first Bible. As a
whole, it is called the "law of Moses" or the "law of the Lord." In existing worship groups, it is called the Torah or the Pentateuch. Whatever the
moniker, it is a history, the only revelation of the character of God backed
by such a multitude of historic evidence! God's covenanting love oozes out
of every page on behalf of all people, despite their behavior! Today we are

to have the inner desire to respond with love! By naming these five books the Pentateuch, though, we subtly help the public gloss over the validity of their being history.

Behold, the incomprehensible God chose to communicate to us to the extent he wanted us to understand. And there are more pages ahead!

We are keenly aware of God as sovereign over everything. We are thrilled that our Lord God is over all people. We are born in that love and are also born with an inner being of self-as-god, which needs God's help!

We've read only 15 percent of the whole Book. Besides learning from trained leadership, learn to learn by your reading the Book. Continue at home with confidence, reading all the pages of "God's answering service"! By believing, you become one of God's treasured possessions in his unfailing love.

A reader asks God,

"Me, not an Israelite, loved by you, Lord God?"

"Yes, you."

"Me!"

REGULATIONS AND REVELATIONS
JOSHUA TO ESTHER

FROM JOSHUA

*T*HE LORD HAD TOLD MOSES that Joshua would be the next leader. We frequently tout Moses and barely tell of Joshua, except regarding Jericho—and that often is for the children. Here is God's introduction to Joshua, or really it is his commission for service:

> Get ready to cross the Jordan River into the land . . . as I promised Moses . . . No one will be able to stand up against you . . . As I was with Moses, so I will be with you; I will never leave you nor forsake you. Be strong and courageous . . . to inherit the land . . . Be strong and very courageous . . . Obey all the law . . . that you may be successful wherever you go . . . Do everything written in it. Then you will be prosperous and successful . . . Be strong and courageous . . . Do not be discouraged, for the Lord your God will be with you wherever you go. (Josh. 1:2–9)

Did Joshua wonder, *What lies ahead in my life that you, Lord God, need to be so emphatic?*

Joshua sent two men across the Jordan as spies. Rahab protected them and gave a testimony on behalf of her people that they were well aware of God's guidance that had thrust them out of Egypt and brought them across the Red Sea: "Our hearts melted in fear and everyone's courage failed because of you, for the Lord your God is God in heaven above and on the earth below" (Josh. 2:11). Note the claim "above" and "below." The men assured Rahab of protection for her and her family.

As the leaders stood in the edge of the flooding Jordan River, it stopped flowing and the bed became dry ground! People and animals crossed safely! We wonder how many. Afterward, the river resumed its flooding. Twelve stones were set as a memorial "so that all the peoples of the earth might know that the hand of the Lord is powerful and so that you might always fear the Lord your God" (Josh. 4:24). Tradespeople who later saw the memorial and understood its meaning would have told it to others.

The Lord gave explicit direction for the approach to Jericho. The Israelites obeyed. They shouted. Walls collapsed. They killed all people and animals, saving only Rahab and her kin. They burned the whole city. One Israelite man who kept items for himself was identified by the Lord, and he and his family were stoned to death.

The Lord directed the destruction of Ai, leaving neither survivors nor fugitives, but keeping livestock and plunder. In the celebration, Joshua read the book of the law as written by Moses.

The Gibeonites deceived Joshua, and he covenanted their security (Josh. 9).

During the battle with the Amorites, Joshua prayed, "Sun, stand still over Gibeon, and you, moon, over the Valley of Aijalon." After Joshua said that, "The sun stood still, and the moon stopped, till the nation avenged itself of its enemies" (Josh. 10:12–13). The sun stopped in midday! "There has never been a day like it before or since, a day when the Lord listened to a human being" (Josh. 10:14).

Thirty-one kings were conquered. "For it was the Lord himself who hardened their hearts to wage war against Israel, so that he might destroy them totally, exterminating them without mercy, as the Lord had commanded Moses" (Josh. 11:20).

We quickly need to recall the preface the Lord had given Moses regarding the people of Canaan: "Destroy all their carved images and their cast idols, and demolish all their high places" (Num. 33:52). Joshua was doing what the Lord required. "Not one of all the Lord's good promises to Israel failed; every one was fulfilled" (Josh. 21:45).

For so many people it was early death for spurning God! Were there some people who secretly loved the Lord God even though they died in a judgment event?

We begin to realize that God's goal for us is not length of this life on earth, but the relationship with God while here. Again, God is Lord, the one who says, "You live," allowing you to continue on this earth, or "You die," resulting in separation from this life.

The land was divided for each tribe, with Ephraim and Manasseh receiving land instead of the tribe of Joseph. The Levites were given towns, and Joshua was given one town. The cities of refuge were assigned.

Joshua followed Moses's example by giving a lengthy farewell address. He reviewed their history with them. He included encouragement and warnings about the foreign gods among them, recording these things in the book of the law of God. Joshua died at the age of 110.

The result of this obedient service was that "Israel served the Lord throughout the lifetime of Joshua and of the elders who outlived him and who had experienced everything the Lord had done for Israel" (Josh. 24:31; cf. Judg. 2:7). That is a rare and high compliment!

Note that God, who establishes life on this earth, is the one who sovereignly directs removal, always on the basis of spurning God.

FROM JUDGES

Leadership will now be by judges.

The next city attacked is significant. The city, Jerusalem, was attacked and put to the sword, with other cities following. Soon there were failures, and quickly the analysis was given:

> I said, "I will never break my covenant with you, and you shall not make a covenant with the people of this land, but you shall break down their altars." Yet you have disobeyed me. Why have you done this? And I have also said, "I will not drive them out before you; they will become traps for you, and their gods will become snares to you." (Judg. 2:1–3)

The foreign god Asherah is noted a few times, Baal is mentioned several times, and Dagon is named once.

> Then the Israelites did evil in the eyes of the Lord and served the Baals. They forsook the Lord, the God of their ancestors . . . They followed and worshiped various gods of the peoples around them . . . The Lord gave them into the hands of raiders . . . He sold them into the hands of their enemies . . . The hand of the Lord was against them to defeat them, just as he had sworn to them. (Judg. 2:11–15)

Eight other times the record in Judges notes the same evil. Several times when a judge led the people to worship the Lord, God granted peace for many years. Thus, the first two chapters of Judges present a vivid, yet sad, introduction to historical events of many years.

Deborah, Gideon, and Samson are often presented in modern drama programs.

Again, no one can point fingers of shame at those people without comparing them with one's own society, including ours. The evidence of God's love continues, as again and again after an "evening" there is a "morning."

FROM RUTH

Listen to the village gossiper at the corner of the lane: "Listen! Woman leaves family and culture for a foreign land and its god!"

Yes, Ruth did just that. After considerable calamity of three deaths in the family, Ruth chose to leave her kin and their gods to go with her mother-in-law, Naomi.

Let us give considerable credit to the deceased father-in-law, Elimelech. The name means "my God is king," and Elimelech was of the Benjamin-Judah group. That strongly implies that he had memorized Scriptures and had endeavored in some limited fashion to offer sacrifices. In a foreign culture, the significant sacrifice would be the fellowship, or peace, offering. Thus, he could reassure his family that by believing the God of Abraham, Isaac, and Jacob, they would have peace with the holy God.

When her mother-in-law announced her return to the homeland, Orpah was polite. Ruth, on the other hand, insisted on going with her. "Don't urge me to leave you . . . Where you go I will go, and where you stay I will stay. Your people will be my people and your God my God" (Ruth 1:16). The father must have given convincing testimony.

Today, knowing the end of all this, we must quickly say that God sovereignly arranged this sequence, including having Ruth follow the gleaners in a field owned by a kinsman, Boaz. As God planned it, Boaz and Ruth fell in love.

A bit of culture was involved at this juncture. Boaz was required to invite the attention of another relative as to the availability of Ruth for remarriage. The writer of Ruth provides dramatic suspense until the moment the other man declined. Boaz and Ruth were married and had a son whom they named Obed.

As the curtain closes on this calamity-romance, the sign in front reads: "Boaz, the father of Obed, the father of Jesse, the father of David" (Ruth 4:22).

God lovingly directs through calamity, although we may not recognize so at the time.

FROM 1 SAMUEL

One of Elkanah's wives, Hannah, was barren and had been teased and misunderstood for some time. She prayed, "Lord Almighty, if you will only look on your servant's misery and remember me, and not forget your servant but give her a son, then I will give him to the Lord for all the days of his life, and no razor will ever be used on his head" (1 Sam. 1:11). The son she soon bore was named Samuel ("heard by God") "because I asked the Lord for him" (1 Sam. 1:20).

As Hannah gave the child to the priest Eli for the Lord's service, she gave a beautiful prayer praising the character of God.

A man of God later confronted Eli regarding his wicked sons. Eli and his family line would come to a close. One night the Lord called to Samuel four times. After the third time, Eli recognized that it was the Lord who had been calling. Samuel was obliged to tell Eli of the judgment upon the family. The Israelites soon lost a battle in which Eli's two sons were killed. Eli died upon hearing the news, just as the Lord had announced! The Lord honored the Israelites over the Philistines.

Samuel had two sons, and neither honored God. As the people recognized Samuel's age and the quality of his sons, they asked for a king "to lead us, such as all the other nations have" (1 Sam. 8:5). The Lord responded, "It is not you they have rejected, but they have rejected me as their king" (1 Sam. 8:7). The Lord directed Samuel to find and anoint Saul. Samuel's farewell address reminded them that failing to obey the Lord would bring disaster.

Saul disobeyed twice, and the Lord rejected him as king, though not just then.

Young David was permitted to confront the giant Goliath, and he did so in the name of the Lord, killing him by sling and stone and with Goliath's own sword. David's success as a military leader quickly resulted in a public chant praising David and disparaging Saul. Jealousy ensued. Saul tried to kill David more than once. Saul's son Jonathan loved David and helped him numerous times. David established a habit of asking the Lord's permission to enter into battle. The Lord affirmed and often pronounced a win.

Twice David had a simple opportunity to kill Saul, but firmly declined.

Romance entered this history as Abigail calmed David's anger regarding her husband, Nabal. Upon the husband's death, David and Abigail were married.

Saul even asked a medium to call upon the soul of Samuel, which she did. Samuel responded in a few words. Saul had disobeyed. The deaths of Saul and his two sons are recorded again.

The record of two contrasting lifestyles is clear. Disobedience brings disaster. Obedience and asking of the Lord brings honor. When Samuel criticized the people for the evil of asking for a king, he encouraged them: "Do not be afraid . . . yet do not turn away from the Lord, but serve the Lord with all your heart . . . For the sake of his great name the Lord will not reject his people, because the Lord was pleased to make you his own" (1 Sam. 12:20–22). Despite their inconsistency, God loved them! Samuel said to Saul, "But now your kingdom will not endure; the Lord has sought out a man after his own heart and appointed him ruler of his people, because you have not kept the Lord's command" (1 Sam. 13:14). Judgment and love are blended together! When selecting David, the Lord cautioned Samuel, "Do not consider his appearance or his height . . . The Lord does not look at the things that people look at. People look at the outward appearance, but the Lord looks at the heart" (1 Sam. 16:7).

How many times does it need to be said and illustrated by lives that the Lord primarily considers one's inner being, or heart, rather than behavior? God loves all. God especially responds to each one who responds to his love!

FROM 2 SAMUEL

David had a time of lament regarding Saul, as referred to in the book of Jashar, a writing outside the Scriptures. That writing was apparently known by the Hebrew people.

"The war between the house of Saul and the house of David lasted a long time. David grew stronger and stronger, while the house of Saul grew weaker and weaker" (2 Sam. 3:1). "David was thirty years old when he became king, and he reigned forty years. In Hebron he reigned over Judah seven years and six months, and in Jerusalem he reigned over all Israel and Judah thirty-three years" (2 Sam. 5:4–5).

God instructed the prophet Nathan to tell David that one of his offspring would build a house for God's dwelling. God told Nathan to give David a message from him:

> I will raise up your offspring to succeed you, your own flesh and blood, and I will establish his kingdom. He is the one who will build a house for my Name, and I will establish the throne of his kingdom forever. I will be his father, and he will be my son . . . But my love will never be taken away from him, as I took it away from Saul . . . Your house and your kingdom will endure forever before me; your throne will be established forever. (2 Sam. 7:12–16)

Later there will be interruptions, but with future finality, Jesus Christ will rule from that throne.

David was blatantly improper with Bathsheba, and he confessed that to a prophet. His confession to God is recorded in Psalm 51. The firstborn son of David and Bathsheba died. Their next child was named Solomon. The Lord loved this child and had declared for him the name Jedidiah, which means "loved by the Lord." A third son of David, Absalom, later conspired against him, even causing disruption. Absalom erected a monument in honor of himself. When Absalom was killed in battle, David grieved bitterly.

David composed and sang a long song of thankfulness and praise to the Lord. The words near the end of the song say, "The Lord lives! Praise be to my Rock! Exalted be my God, the Rock, my Savior! He is the God who avenges me . . . who sets me free from my enemies . . . Therefore I will praise you, Lord, among the nations; I will sing the praises of your name" (2 Sam. 22:47–50).

David did what God did! God continued to love Adam and Eve after they became unlovable, and David continued to love Absalom after he became unlovable.

FROM 1 KINGS

Adonijah, another son of David, and also a conspirator, arose and declared, "I will be king" (1 Kings 1:5). As the matter was politely called to King David's attention, he arranged a public display on behalf of his son Solomon as king. The public response was so great that the ground shook. Solomon had Adonijah killed. That was the honor-shame method of society. David, approaching death, charged Solomon, "Walk in obedience to him, and keep his decrees . . . so that you may prosper in all you do" (1 Kings 2:3).

King David had started to gather materials to build God's temple. God gave King Solomon "wisdom and very great insight, and a breadth of understanding as measureless as the sand on the seashore" (1 Kings 4:29). Five centuries (1 Kings 6:1) after the Israelites had left Egypt and during the fourth year of Solomon's reign, he began to build the temple. Considerable ornate design and specific materials were included. It took seven years to complete the temple, but Solomon took thirteen years to build his palace. Was there a little pride and selfishness there? As the ark of the covenant was properly placed in the temple, a cloud filled the temple, symbolizing God's presence. Was that cloud also intended to be a reminder of the forty-year wandering? King Solomon led the assembly in prayer and praise of God. Numerous animals were sacrificed during the fourteen days of celebration.

Note the solemn reflection: "But will God really dwell on earth?" (1 Kings 8:27). That reflection is also recorded in 2 Chronicles 6:18.

The record jumps toward the end of Solomon's life. Solomon had taken many wives of other nations, even after the Lord's explicit warning. The result was not surprising: he worshiped such gods as Ashtoreth, Molech, and Chemosh. That appeared to be easy for him, for his heart had turned away from the Lord. The Lord's response was disaster—the nation was divided in two, of ten tribes and two tribes. The Lord used human conflict to bring that about. Solomon reigned forty years and died, and all was recorded in a biography.

The northern tribe was named Israel, and Jeroboam became the first king. However, God said to Jeroboam, "I tore the kingdom way from the house of David . . . You have not been like my servant David, who kept my commands and followed me with all his heart, doing only what was right in my eyes. You have done more evil than all who lived before you. You have made for yourself other gods . . . and turned your back on me" (1 Kings 14:8–9).

Kings of the Northern and Southern Kingdoms are listed as doing evil in the eyes of the Lord. Asa, king of Judah, did right for forty-one years, and his son Jehoshaphat did right also.

One day the prophet Elijah challenged the evil northern King Ahab to meet with the Baal prophets on Mount Carmel (1 Kings 18). He told the people, "If the Lord is God, follow him; but if Baal is God, follow him . . . The god who answers by fire—he is God" (18:21, 24). Considerable drama took place throughout the day until Elijah prayed, "Answer me, Lord, answer me, so these people will know that you, Lord, are God, and that you are turning their hearts back again" (18:37). God's fire fell, burning the entire sacrifice and setting! The people responded in chorus, "The Lord—he is God!" (18; 39). Elijah had the Baal prophets killed. The three-year drought was broken by heavy rain.

The drama continued, for when Elijah fled, he hid in a cave. He lamented that he seemed to be the only believer. The Lord gently encouraged him: "Yet I reserve seven thousand in Israel—all whose knees have not bowed down to Baal and whose mouths have not kissed him" (1 Kings 19:18). Amazingly, there were seven thousand secret believers in the Northern Kingdom! God knows our hearts. He is the final judge.

King Ahab continued in evil ways, yet one day he humbled himself. The Lord directed Elijah to inform him that disaster would come upon his son instead of upon him. Finally, King Ahab was wounded in battle and died.

God allowed leaders to use free will in a self-as-god manner. We find that God's love for people includes immense patience. Both are evident in our society today.

FROM 2 KINGS

Continuing now through the book of 2 Kings, we see that God used extensive drama. Elijah walked to three towns, as though to leave Elisha, who resolutely walked along. At the Jordan, Elijah parted the water for a dry-ground crossing. As a chariot of fire and horses of fire appeared, Elijah was swept up in a whirlwind—to heaven! Enoch and Elijah did not die a natural human death. Elisha then used Elijah's cloak to part the river.

Elisha performed several miracles, but the cure for a pagan military leader, Naaman, is often dramatized today. A Hebrew slave girl encouraged Naaman to visit the prophet Elisha. Upon a humiliating submersion in the Jordan River, Naaman was healed of his leprosy. He said, "Now I know that there is no God in all the world except in Israel" (2 Kings 5:15). However, he added a caveat. He requested that God would forgive him for entering the temple of Rimmon with his master and bowing down. Without scolding Naaman,

Elisha responded, "Go in peace" (5:18–19). Elisha's helper, Gehazi, was given leprosy for lying (2 Kings 5:20–27).

Elisha asked God for other miracles, which were evident to many people and individuals, and none were for his own benefit.

Joash, king of Judah (Southern Kingdom), was allowed to reign for forty years and "did what was right in the eyes of the Lord" (2 Kings 12:2). However, he did not completely do right, as he allowed the high places to be used for sacrifices. The illustration is that pleasing God does not require perfect conduct. Azariah did right and was allowed to reign fifty-two years. Time and again, there was inconsistency. The people forsook the Lord and worshiped idols and nature. They sacrificed their sons and daughters in the fire. They practiced divination and sorcery. They worshiped the Lord, but also imitated the customs of the nations from which they had come (see 2 Kings 17, for example). God was patient.

During the reign of Hezekiah, king of Judah (Southern Kingdom), God judged Israel (Northern Kingdom). "The king of Assyria deported Israel to Assyria" (2 Kings 18:11).

Upon imminent attack, Isaiah gave the Lord's message to Hezekiah: "For out of Jerusalem will come a remnant, and out of Mount Zion a band of survivors . . . I will defend this city and save it, for my sake and for the sake of David my servant" (2 Kings 19:31, 34). What happened? "That night the angel of the Lord went out and put to death a hundred and eighty-five thousand in the Assyrian camp. When the people got up the next morning—there were all the dead bodies!" (2 Kings 19:35). What other god had they been worshiping?

Note that God tolerated free will in Manasseh, who did evil all throughout his fifty-five years of reign over Judah!

Josiah did right when the book of the law was found. "He read in their hearing all the words of the Book of the Covenant . . . and renewed the covenant in the presence of the Lord—to follow the Lord and keep his commands . . . with all his heart and all his soul . . . Then all the people pledged themselves to the covenant" (2 Kings 23:2–3).

Battles of victory and of defeat were recorded in the annals of the kings.

When Nebuchadnezzar, king of Babylon, advanced upon Jerusalem, the leadership surrendered. He took the furnishings of the temple and carried into exile the leadership, skilled workers, and others—a total of ten thousand people—leaving only the poor (2 Kings 24:14–16). "So Judah went into captivity, away from her land" (2 Kings 25:21).

God is not whimsical in judgment. God does not require perfection or consistency. God requires love from one's heart. God's love is unfailing!

FROM 1 CHRONICLES

First Chronicles begins with Adam and continues with many genealogies and assignments, and then it details the adult life of David. The Hebrew Bible has Chronicles as the last book.

In the midst of battles, David stopped to praise God:

Sing to the Lord, all the earth;

    proclaim his salvation day after day . . .

Give thanks to the Lord, for he is good;

    his love endures forever.

    . . . that we may give thanks to your holy name,

    and glory in your praise.

Praise be to the Lord, the God of Israel,

    from everlasting to everlasting.

               (1 Chron. 16:23, 34–36, in Hebrew poetry form)

God promised David, "I will raise up your offspring to succeed you, one of your own sons, and I will establish his kingdom . . . I will establish his throne forever. I will be his father, and he will be my son. I will never take my love away from him . . . His throne will be established forever" (1 Chron. 17:11–14).

"God sent an angel to destroy Jerusalem." Note that the verse does not say "completely destroy" as had been the case for other cultures. The Lord became grieved and said, "Enough! Withdraw your hand" (1 Chron. 21:15).

In his charge to Solomon, God again asserted, "He will be my son, and I will be his father. And I will establish the throne of his kingdom over Israel forever" (1 Chron. 22:10). Later, a caveat is included: "I will establish his kingdom forever if he is unswerving" (1 Chron. 28:7).

David ruled for forty years over Israel. He ruled over the northern group for seven years and the united northern and southern kingdoms for thirty-three. "As for the events of King David's reign, from beginning to end, they are written in the records of Samuel the seer, the records of Nathan the prophet and the records of Gad the seer" (1 Chron. 29:29).

FROM 2 CHRONICLES

This opens with Solomon unselfishly asking God for help as king, and God blessed him immensely. Solomon had also asked a neighbor for materials and craftsmen to build a temple. With the ark in its proper place, an extensive celebration of more than a week took place. The biblical record again notes Solomon's humility as the temple was filled with God's glory: "But will God really dwell on earth with humans?" (2 Chron. 6:18; also 1 Kings 8:27). Would God again dwell on earth in some humanlike form as at first, as with Adam and Eve? The fire that came down from heaven was God's answer of his sovereign presence. Later at night the Lord appeared, but in what form?

It is appreciated that many events were recorded in the Book twice, for two witnesses of the same testimony are accepted as valid.

Sometimes God troubled people with "every kind of distress" (2 Chron. 15:6). Those who did not seek the Lord were to be killed. At times, the neighboring countries feared the God of Israel.

We need to accept that God intervenes in our societies today, although not always so conspicuously. Smile as you read that "God has the power to help or to overthrow" (2 Chron. 25:8).

Many of the Southern Kingdom kings obeyed God. Uzziah did well until his pride arose. King Josiah was an excellent example. He removed the idols. When the book of the law, or book of the covenant, was found, he assembled the people and read "all the words," pledging the people to follow God (2 Chron. 34:30). He also provided the animals for the Passover.

However, Nebuchadnezzar of Babylon destroyed Jerusalem and the temple and took the people into exile. That exile would last seventy years, according to the foretelling of Jeremiah (Jer. 29:10). Later, Cyrus of Persia would bid the people to return (2 Chron. 36:23; Ezra 1:1–3).

FROM EZRA

The first chapter of Ezra states, "The Lord, the God of heaven, has given me [Cyrus] all the kingdoms of the earth and he has appointed me to build a temple for him at Jerusalem in Judah. Any of his people among you may go up to Jerusalem in Judah and build the temple of the Lord, the God of Israel, the God who is in Jerusalem" (Ezra 1:2–4). Neighbors gave valuables and livestock. Cyrus handed over to them the furnishings that had been in the temple.

About fifty thousand Jews returned to Jerusalem and commenced by building the altar and sacrificing for the Feast of Tabernacles. Others made several attempts to stop the Jews (the name used by neighboring nations) from building the temple. The earthly struggle was obvious. Was there also, unseen by people, an attempt by Satan through humans to hinder the progress? The building was encouraged by the preaching of Haggai and Zechariah and the instructions from the book of Moses regarding the Passover. The estimate is that they finished in about two decades and had an installation according to the law of the Lord.

Ezra had also returned and immediately started teaching. Even the foreign king Artaxerxes sent encouragement. Ezra gave credit to the hand of God by fasting and prayers. Intermarriage with foreign women had happened again.

FROM NEHEMIAH

Nehemiah states that he is still in exile. For those who had returned, he uttered intense prayer: "Lord, let your ear be attentive to the prayer of this your servant and to the prayer of your servants who delight in revering your name" (Neh. 1:11). God was gracious in sending Nehemiah back, and he immediately began directing the rebuilding of the walls and gates. There was outside opposition and internal difficulty because many of their own were poor. Some of the men had a weapon in one hand and a tool in the other. The walls were completed within two months, as recognized by outsiders: "Our enemies lost their self-confidence, because they realized that this work had been done with the help of our God" (Neh. 6:16). About fifty thousand people had returned. Day after day, Ezra read from the book of the law of God. The people assembled for confession and praising God for being everlasting, compassionate, and continuing with the covenant of love. Ezra assembled two grand choirs for dedicating the rebuilt wall (Neh. 12).

FROM ESTHER

The book of Esther presents a drama of free will and obedience, compassion and hatred, suspense and confirmation.

In a drama presentation, the curtain opens. In the midst of the reign of Xerxes, king of Persia, a countrywide celebration was held. Widespread tension arose when the queen refused to dance at the request of the king. That was a grave violation of the husband-wife relationship in the culture.

Esther, cousin of Mordecai, who had not revealed that she was Jewish, was selected to replace Vashti as queen. *Curtain closes.*

Curtain opens. Mordecai had revealed an assassination plot against the king, and it was properly recorded in the annals with credit. Haman, a high official, did not receive honor from Mordecai, and his anger rose to where he bribed the king to have the Jews in the land killed. The king lent his ring for Haman to write such a law, which he did! It was properly issued. *Curtain closes.*

Curtain opens. Jews all across the country were in mourning. Mordecai, from the gate, begged Queen Esther to plead with the king, her husband, for mercy for the Jews. Esther succinctly reminded Mordecai that approaching the king without being summoned might result in death.

Mordecai continued, pulling out all stops: "If you remain silent at this time, relief and deliverance for the Jews will arise from another place, but you and your father's family will perish. And who knows but that you have come to your royal position for such a time as this?" (Est. 4:14). Esther, trusting God, bid the Jews to fast with her for three days and then, she said, "I will go to the king, even though it is against the law. And if I perish, I perish" (Est. 4:16). *Curtain closes.*

Curtain opens. Esther had a banquet for the king and Haman. Haman had built a gallows intended for Mordecai. God caused the king to have a restless sleep, which the king used to read the chronicles of the previous assassination plot. Behold, at day break, the king commanded Haman to show the city gratitude for Mordecai by means of Haman's servitude! Friends warned Haman. What's next? *Curtain closes.*

Curtain opens. At the queen's second banquet for the king and Haman, she explained that the purpose for all this was to beg for mercy for her people, who had been sold for slaughter and annihilation.

"Who is behind this?"

"Haman."

Haman "shot himself in the foot" by appearing to molest the queen. The king responded with a crescendo: "Hang him on Haman's gallows!" *Curtain closes.*

Curtain opens. The king directed Mordecai to issue a decree, and Mordecai composed one that said all the Jews were to defend themselves, kill attackers, and take plunder. All the Jews were joyful. "And many people of other nationalities became Jews because fear of the Jews had seized them" (Est. 8:17). The Jews killed hundreds and thousands of their enemies, but did not take plunder. *Curtain closes.*

Mordecai directed all Jews to celebrate the special day that had been chosen by lot, and hence it was named Purim (*pur* means "the lot"). Mordecai was raised to second in command to the king.

Many regulations have been given for this new nation of Israel, and many are the notations of the consequences of obeying or not. God allows free will. Some people trust God. God's love is obvious for those who wish to love the Lord. God is sovereign!

We have read seventeen books of the Book, and we readily believe God's unfailing love and the evidences of self-as-god people. However, since the flood, there appears to be a bias. Little encouragement for the rest of humanity has been presented. Soon after the time of Christ Jesus, while the early Christian leadership was choosing material for a second testament, they changed the sequence of the books for their use. First and Second Chronicles, then one book, was moved much earlier. Job was moved from near the end of the Hebrew Bible to much earlier. The Jews retained their sequence.

Prepare for a startling transition!

THE MAN, THE BULK OF HUMANITY

JOB

JOB, THE "IGNORANT"!

THE BOOK OF JOB does not contain the words listed below though they occurred frequently in the writings pertaining to the Israelites. Apparently, Job was ignorant of their oral history and writings. A discussion of this will be presented next.

- Abraham, Isaac, Jacob
- Adam and Eve
- Atonement
- Baal, Ashtoreth, Chemosh, Molech
- Book of the law
- Cities (named)
- Covenant (God's)
- Commandments, the Ten
- Egypt
- Gentile
- Hebrew
- Israel(ites)
- Jerusalem
- Jew

- Kings (named)
- Moses
- Sovereign

Obviously, Job was not an Israelite. Hence, Job represents the bulk of humanity that was not part of the Israelite culture.

There is considerable argument as to the date of the book of Job and of Job himself. Sufficient, though, for this book is to say that the person lived centuries before Christ Jesus. Also, Job lived 140 years after God blessed him again (Job 42:16), and so whatever the total number of years was, it matches the somewhat long lives of those who lived during the centuries just after the flood.

FROM JOB

A moment of review. After the flood, there were different languages and cultures. Several books of the Book we have just read record that considerable attention was given to one culture. The purpose was to present that culture as an example to the world. The cultures that ignored God received several judgments. Had there been a positive appeal to the rest of the world? We have been pondering that. This section is a consideration of Job in the context of the whole Book.

Many believers approach the book of Job as a lesson on how to handle adversity. We'll consider that in the last paragraph of this section.

The text opens with Job giving sacrifices on behalf of his family. Evidently Job had learned that much from the oral history passed down from Adam and Eve that God's plan was the substitution of an animal's life in place of a human life.

We don't need to know Job's genealogy or the town of birth; we just need to know that Job was blameless in his society and feared God. He honored his family and God. One day, angels and Satan (the accuser) appeared with the Lord, who challenged Satan by asking where he came from. This is a teaching moment, for of course God knew all about Satan, but he asked such a question so that we would have the answer. Satan answered, "From roaming throughout the earth, going back and forth on it" (Job 1:7). This wording alerts us that Satan's capability was well beyond human ability. As the Lord praised Job to Satan, he replied that of course Job would be faithful to God because of all the blessings already given to Job. The Lord responded to Satan, "Everything he has is in your power, but on the man himself do not lay a finger" (Job 1:12).

Shortly afterward, messengers announced that Job's herds had been destroyed and his family had been killed. Job had not been part of the previous conversation, yet he reacted with emotion and worship: "The Lord gave and the Lord has taken away; may the name of the Lord be praised" (Job 1:21). Note that Job said *the Lord*, and not *God*. Job recognized God's right to continue or shorten one's earth-life.

At a second council consisting of angels, Satan, and God, God directly challenged Satan to consider Job, largely because he was one who feared God and maintained integrity: "Very well, then, he is in your hands; but you must spare his life" (Job 2:6). Satan immediately afflicted Job with painful sores from top to bottom. Job's wife recommended that Job should "Curse God and die!" (Job 2:9). Job, however, did not sin against the Lord.

Three friends from a distance met and approached Job, barely recognizing him. They observed his suffering for seven days without saying a word. Job spoke, cursing the day of his birth. Eliphaz, Bildad, and Zophar took turns speaking to Job, allowing him to respond each time. Their thoughts were undoubtedly common in their society, and we recognize them in ours today. A repeating theme was that Job was being judged for being secretly at fault. Another thought was that no one can understand God. We'll gloss over the presentations of these three men.

Listen to Job's humanity and especially to his clarity of faith in what he says:

- My joy in unrelenting pain—that I had not denied the words of the Holy One. (6:10)
- Teach me, and I will be quiet. (6:24)
- I could only plead with my Judge for mercy . . . If only there were someone to mediate between us, someone to bring us together. (9:15, 33)
- If I am guilty—woe to me! Even if I am innocent, I cannot lift my head, for I am full of shame. (10:15)
- But I desire to speak to the Almighty and to argue my case with God . . . Though he slay me, yet will I hope in him. (13:3, 15)
- Then summon me and I will answer, or let me speak, and you reply to me. (13:22)
- If someone dies, will they live again? . . . I will wait for my renewal to come . . . You will long for the creature your hands have made . . . My offenses will be sealed up in a bag; you will cover over my sin. (14:14–17)
- Even now my witness is in heaven; my advocate is on high. My intercessor is my friend. (16:19–20)
- Give me, O God, the pledge you demand. Who else will put up security for me? (17:3)
- I know that my redeemer lives, and that in the end he will stand on the earth . . . Yet in my flesh I will see God . . . How my heart yearns within me! (19:25–27)
- The fear of the Lord—that is wisdom. (28:28)
- What will I do when God confronts me? What will I answer when called to account? (31:14)

Job demonstrates that an ordinary person, without understanding many details, can trust God!

Another friend, Elihu (not one of the other Elihus recorded in the Book), identified as being younger, had waited for the proper moment to speak. He chided the other three and then addressed Job:

For God does speak—now one way, now another . . . Or someone may be chastened on a bed of pain . . . Yet if there is an angel at their side, a messenger . . . to tell them how to be upright . . . I have found a ransom for them . . . If it were his intention and he withdrew his spirit and breath, all humanity would perish together and mankind would return to the dust . . . Should God then reward you on your terms, when you refuse to repent? . . . If you sin, how does that affect him? . . . If you are righteous, what do you give to him? . . . I will ascribe justice to my Maker . . . He is wooing you from the laws of distress . . . But now you are laden with the judgment due the wicked . . . God is exalted in his power . . . How great is God—beyond our understanding . . . God's voice thunders in marvelous ways; he does great things beyond our understanding . . . We cannot draw up our case because of our darkness . . . Therefore, people revere him. (Excerpts from Job 32–37)

It appears to us that God had directed Elihu as a prophet.

The Lord spoke clearly to Job: "I will question you . . . Have you comprehended the vast expanses of the earth? . . . Can you set up God's dominion over the earth?" (Job 38:3, 18, 33). "Will the one who contends with the Almighty correct him?" (Job 40:2). There are no commandments and no sacrifices, but only an elaborate review of this earth that our awesome Creator-God provided for us and an explanation that God is sovereign! How loving God is, and hence he has given us evidence to elicit our love in return. Job confessed that he was unworthy.

The Lord continued to present the disparity between God and humanity.

We, too, can bring our questions to God in humility and join with Job: "Surely I spoke of things I did not understand, things too wonderful for me to know . . . My ears had heard of you but now my eyes have seen you" (Job 42:3–5).

God blessed Job with another family and a "second half of life."

When the Book is used as a catalogue of topics such as adversity, Job is the reference par excellence. And God's unfailing love continues.

We have an illustration that God delights in hearing the cry from one's inner being (soul, heart) for an advocate, mediator, or redeemer. It is a cry that God is just and merciful and loving in the midst of whatever happens on earth. Job's cry amounts to a desire for a future in God's presence when God will be fully understood. He is not selfishly crying out for restoration of assets and family, but he desires what neither he nor any other human can provide. He has confidence that somehow God will provide, as he did with the first animal on behalf of Adam and Eve. Any person in any part of the world can plead in the same manner without having had any human religious schooling. That is the supreme use of free will! Such a person does not fear death, or separation from earth-life.

Add assurance from the New Testament: "Come near to God and he will come near to you" (James 4:8). "If we confess our sins, he is faithful and just and will forgive us our sins and purify us from all unrighteousness" (1 John 1:9). We will understand later that this is by Christ Jesus.

Any response from God of additional blessings in your life after an adversity may or may not be visible and measurable, as it was with Job. This is good news for all humanity, and immediately more so for the millions of people today who are being subjected to starvation or any other likelihood of a short life, or those who are imbedded in a culture of fear. May they cry out for an advocate, even if they have not heard of Christ Jesus. Those imbedded in a religion need to call upon this God—creator and lover.

A reader asks God,

"Me, as an ignorant one, loved by you, Lord God?"

"Yes, you."

"Me!"

PRAISES AND HUMILITY

PSALMS TO SONG OF SONGS

FROM THE PSALMS

THIS IS A COLLECTION from several authors, mostly arranged by author, but not necessarily identified with a particular event. It appears they were circulated in a cluster of five books:

Book One: Psalms 1–41

Book Two: Psalms 42–72

Book Three: Psalms 73–89

Book Four: Psalms 90–106

Book Five: Psalms 107–150

The subject is not calm narration, but personal emotion. Some psalms have been used for group worship. Many sentences are memorized for praise and comfort. Some were the result of specific events. The literary form is consistently Hebrew poetry. That style consists of couplets of two statements that repeat or add a slight enhancement. The titles are numbered with the verse numbers in the Hebrew text, but not so in English.

Bless and *blessed* are frequent in Book One and Book Five. Who blesses whom, how is one blessed, and why?

Psalm 1 defines and contrasts a blessed person with a wicked one. Psalm 2 states God's decree for life: "You are my son; today I have become your father" (Ps. 2:7) and "Serve the Lord with fear . . . Blessed are all who take refuge in him" (Ps. 2:11–12). Together, these two chapters form a prologue for the whole book of Psalms.

Book One, as defined above, consists of Psalms 1–41. Many of David's expressions are thanks for God's protection from enemies. God is repeatedly described as righteous and merciful. David's confidence is firm: "The Lord reigns forever" (Ps. 9:7). David is confident in his future: "I will be vindicated and will see your face; when I awake, I will be satisfied with seeing your likeness" (Ps. 17:15). Psalm 19 is full of praise and humility, opening with "The heavens declare the glory of God." Psalm 22 begins with words Christ Jesus used when on his cross: "My God, my God, why have you forsaken me?" (Ps. 22:1). Multitudes quote the entire twenty-third psalm, which begins, "The Lord is my shepherd, I lack nothing."

The Lord gives strength to his people. The Lord blesses his people with peace. Psalm 34 tells us that "The angel of the Lord encamps around those who fear him" (Ps. 34:7) and "The eyes of the Lord are on the righteous, and his ears are attentive to their cry" (Ps. 34:15). We also appreciate the affirmation, "But the Lord laughs at the wicked, for he knows their day is coming" (Ps. 37:13). Christ Jesus is seen in Psalm 40:7: "Then I said, 'Here I am, I have come—it is written about me in the scroll'" (Luke 4:20). The conclusion is anticipated: "Praise be to the Lord, the God of Israel, from everlasting to everlasting. Amen and Amen" (Ps. 41:13).

In Book Two (Psalms 42–72), the author is quite emotional. "My soul thirsts for God, for the living God. When can I go and meet with God?" (Ps. 42:2). Anyone in adversity can benefit from Psalm 46:10: "Be still, and know that I am God." Praise God that even though "the ransom for a life is costly, no payment is ever enough . . . God will redeem me from the realm of the dead; he will surely take me to himself" (Ps. 49:8, 15). David's personal confession is in Psalm 51. Here is a wish: "Oh, that salvation for Israel would come out of Zion!" (Ps. 53:6). There is testimony: "My soul finds rest in God; my salvation comes from him" (Ps. 62:1). An unselfish concern is "that your ways may be known on earth, your salvation among all nations" (Ps. 67:2). The conclusion is that "All nations will be blessed through him . . . Praise be to his glorious name forever; may the whole earth be filled with his glory. Amen and Amen" (Ps. 72:17, 19).

The psalms in Book Three (Psalms 73–89) are written by or presented by their director of music, Asaph. It surely must have been majestic to have heard these emotions sung by a large group along with their instruments. Psalm 80 is a form of repentance, pleading for a face-to-face restoration with God. Psalm 89 is different; after a few words of speaking for himself, suddenly the psalmist gives a long quotation (verses 19–37) of things God had said, perhaps at various times. The book ends in the familiar tenor: "Praise be to the Lord forever! Amen and Amen" (Ps. 89:52).

Book Four (Psalms 90–106) includes several authors, some of whom are not identified. Psalm 96 is a favorite. You and I are included in this whole purpose: "Let this be written for a future generation, that a people not yet created may praise the Lord" (Ps. 102:18). David raised the emotional level in Psalm 103 with "Praise the Lord, my soul." Psalm 106 also has much excitement: "Praise be to the Lord God of Israel, from everlasting to everlasting. Let all the people say, 'Amen!' Praise the Lord" (Ps. 106:18).

In Book Five (Psalms 107–150), we rejoice with those who celebrate the Passover. Psalms 113–118 are given the title *Hallel*—"Praise." Psalm 119 is separated into twenty-two paragraphs of eight verses, with the first word of each verse of each paragraph beginning with a successive letter of the Hebrew alphabet. We often quote Psalm 121:2: "My help comes from the Lord, the Maker of heaven and earth." Psalm 130 tells us that everyone is a sinner, yet forgiveness and redemption can be claimed. Psalm 136 requires a narrator, with a large vocal choir responding twenty-six times to the narrator with, "His love endures forever!" When did that thought begin? It began on page one of the Book. Confession and humility are included at the end of Psalm 139: "Search me, God, and know my heart; test me and know my anxious thoughts. See if there is any offensive way in me, and lead me in the way everlasting" (Ps. 139:23–24).

Psalms 146–150 were all from David, and they are constant praise of the Lord. That cluster forms a beautiful epilogue for the entire book of Psalms. Besides using vocal praise, Psalm 150 tells us that we can add all our instruments, concluding with, "Let everything that has breath praise the Lord. Praise the Lord" (Ps. 150:6).

Each reader of this book would have chosen selections a little differently. Hundreds of verses have been memorized. Read all 150 Psalms in your Bible!

Stand with tears of joy, kneel in silence with tears of humility— or do both!

We already highlighted that "His love endures forever." Another phrase that needs to be thrust forth is "unfailing love." That phrase occurs thirty-two times throughout the Psalms. The repetition has the same intention as when a mother tells her child, "I've told you a thousand times."

Yes, you were born in God's love, and you cannot undo continuing love:

unfailing love (6:4)

unfailing love (13:5)

unfailing love (18:50)

unfailing love (21:7)

unfailing love (26:3)

unfailing love (31:6)

unfailing love (32:10)

unfailing love (33:5, 18, 22)

unfailing love (36:7)

unfailing love (42:26)

unfailing love (48:9)

unfailing love (51:1)

unfailing love (52:8)

unfailing love (62:12)

unfailing love (77:8)

unfailing love (85:7)

unfailing love (90:14)

unfailing love (94:18)

unfailing love (107:8, 15, 21, 31)

unfailing love (109:26)

unfailing love (119:41, 76, 88)

unfailing love (130:7)

unfailing love (138:2)

unfailing love (143:8, 12)

unfailing love (147:11)

Amen!

With "His love endures forever" repeated twenty-six times in Psalm 136, and this repetition of "unfailing love," it is no surprise that we will later read that "God is love" (1 John 4:8). That is no casual caption for the character of God. It is integral on every page of the Book, beginning on page one!

What is your emotional response?

FROM PROVERBS

Proverbs is addressed to men. It is about behavior. Women can smile about this type of attention being part of the canon. Men, read Proverbs by yourself and admit that you, like all other men, are fragile. Proverbs was written in Hebrew poetic couplet form, often giving a contrast. Most of the proverbs are credited to Solomon. Did he write them after he had the many women as wives? The purpose of the book is for wisdom and discipline.

"The fear of the Lord is the beginning of knowledge, but fools despise wisdom and instruction" (Prov. 1:7).

Below we read only a few bits of advice from Proverbs.

Father to son:

- Listen, my son, to your father's instruction and do not forsake your mother's teaching. (Prov. 1:8)
- Wisdom will save you from the ways of wicked men. (Prov. 2:12)
- Trust in the Lord with all your heart and lean not on your own understanding. (Prov. 3:5)
- Above all else, guard your heart, for everything you do flows from it. (Prov. 4:23)
- For your ways are in full view of the Lord. (Prov. 5:21)
- But a man who commits adultery has no sense; whoever does so destroys himself. (Prov. 6:32)
- Wisdom speaks as God. (Chapter 8)
- The fear of the Lord adds length to life. (Prov. 10:27)
- The eyes of the Lord are everywhere, keeping watch on the wicked and the good. (Prov. 15:3)
- All a person's ways seem pure to them, but motives are weighed by the Lord. (Prov. 16:2)
- The Lord works out everything to its proper end—even the wicked for a day of disaster. (Prov. 16:4)
- A cheerful heart is good medicine. (Prov. 17:22)
- A prudent wife is from the Lord. (Prov. 19:14)
- Do not boast about tomorrow, for you do not know what a day may bring. (Prov. 27:1)
- Where there is no revelation, people cast off restraint. (Prov. 29:18)

Scattered throughout are reminders of God's love:

- Let love and faithfulness never leave you. (Prov. 3:3)
- I love those who love me, and those who seek me find me. (Prov. 8:17)
- Through love and faithfulness sin is atoned for. (Prov. 16:6)
- What a person desires is unfailing love. (Prov. 19:22)

Lastly, maybe a dear wife had been looking over her husband's shoulder and said, "Dear, please include material about a godly wife." Whatever was the actual case, we have Proverbs chapter 31! "A woman who fears the Lord is to be praised" (Prov. 31:30). (I say this with tears about my wife, Lois, wishing I had done so profusely.)

May each man say, "Thank you, Lord, for these proverbs."

FROM ECCLESIASTES

The text of the book of Ecclesiastes indicates that this book is a declaration of King Solomon.

Let's choose a dramatic setting for Ecclesiastes: The house lights go dim. The spotlight is on the center curtain. A hush. A dramatic several-second pause. The billing had been simple: "King Solomon." Many present had recently been reading his proverbs. Will he start with "Praise the Lord!"? The curtains open slowly, presenting brilliance and gentle colors upon his elegant robes. He raises both arms in a wide arc as if enclosing something, and all we hear is:

"Meaningless, meaningless, meaningless, meaningless."

Now on with the text. Solomon certainly has a caption for his topic. His key word, *meaningless*, is recorded more than thirty times. Everything is meaningless, including wisdom, knowledge, laughter, and life. All is meaningless, a "chasing after the wind" (Eccl. 2:11). Toil is a gift of God. "I know that everything God does will endure forever; nothing can be added to it and nothing taken from it. God does it so that people will fear him"

(Eccl. 3:14). "Who knows if the human spirit rises upward and if the spirit of the animal goes down into the earth?" (Eccl. 3:21). "Indeed, there is no one on earth who is righteous, no one who does what is right and never sins" (Eccl. 7:20). "So no one has power over the time of their death" (Eccl. 8:8). "So you cannot understand the work of God, the Maker of all things" (Eccl. 11:5).

"Now all has been heard; here is the conclusion of the matter: Fear God and keep his commandments, for this is the duty of all mankind. For God will bring every deed into judgment, including every hidden thing, whether it is good or evil" (Eccl. 12:13–14).

This flattens one's ego and enhances one's reciprocating love of God.

Thank you, Lord, that your love has provided this critique of life. It is a critique of any culture. It is an attitude appropriate for any culture.

FROM SONG OF SONGS

Song of Songs has received a swirl of thoughts from time of old to the present. This book presents one man and one woman in love, without certainty as to names. Then what is the lesson? Yes, they were in love when separate and in love when together.

A first thought is that God approves of one man and one woman being in love, ready to be married and have a family. This is no surprise, for God put Adam and Eve together. The second possible thought is that this is allegorical. In that system, specific items figuratively represent some other person or event. Hence it can be thought that this represents the constant unswerving love God has for those who love him. Others pose this book as Solomon's experience with a particular woman.

Love is basic in human life on earth. The man-woman sexual relationship is not evil. Why are we surprised that love is basic in the God-person relationship? That love will be different in God's presence in the future!

We have frequent praise because God's love is constant.

ISAIAH TO MALACHI

FROM ISAIAH

*T*HE BOOK HAS GIVEN US several portions of history, followed by some portions that admit human emotions. This portion, beginning with Isaiah, emphasizes the future from seven centuries before Christ Jesus appeared. Isaiah saw visions during the reigns of four kings (including Ahaz), which are estimated to have covered at least a half century! Of note is "that day," which is scattered throughout Isaiah forty-four times. Several kinds of future events are referenced, and difficulty often arises as to whether the near future or the very distant future is intended. We call such declarations of God's will *prophecy*. Isaiah is the first of several longer prophetic writings, which are followed by several shorter writings regarding the future. There is considerable repetition of two words, *save* and *salvation* (more than a dozen times each). Also, the connective *therefore* flags our attention on many pages.

Isaiah shouts for attention: "Hear me, you heavens! Listen, earth! For the Lord has spoken" (Isa. 1:2). Isaiah further clamors for attention by using *listen* more than thirty times. He begins by speaking for God with a critique of this new nation. Note the terms used in the evaluation of the people: "rebelled," "not understand," "corrupt," "forsaken the Lord," "turned their backs," etc. On the other hand, despite the terms above, "'Come now, let us settle the matter,' says the Lord. 'Though your sins are like scarlet, they shall be as white as snow'" (Isa. 1:18). That is good news of God's love! How?

Here is some of what Isaiah "saw":

> In the last days the mountain of the Lord's temple will be established as the highest of the mountains . . . They will beat their swords into plowshares and their spears into pruning hooks . . . The Lord alone will be exalted in that day, and the idols will totally disappear . . . People will flee . . . from the fearful presence of the Lord and the splendor of his majesty, when he rises to shake the earth. (Isa. 2)

That is confidence for us! This much seems to be a broad introduction. Details follow: "In that day the Branch of the Lord will be beautiful and glorious, . . . glory of the survivors in Israel" (Isa. 4:2). "He lifts up a banner for the distant nations, he whistles for those at the ends of the earth" (Isa. 5:26). Wow! God loves all people, not just this new nation! On another day Isaiah saw "the King, the Lord Almighty" and received assurance that "your guilt is taken away and your sin atoned for" (Isa. 6:5–7). The Hebrew language often presents the future as though it has already happened. That is assurance for us that it is as good as done. My sin is already satisfactorily taken care of, even if I don't yet know the details.

One day Isaiah had an audience with Ahaz, the wicked king of Judah, who was fearful of invasion. Isaiah suggested that Ahaz ask the Lord God for a sign. Ahaz declined. Isaiah continued, "Therefore the Lord himself will give you a sign: The virgin will conceive and give birth to a son, and will call him Immanuel" (Isa. 7:14). A pregnant woman will properly be called a virgin! As only God could present a pregnant woman, so only God could spare Jerusalem! No response by Ahaz is recorded. Maybe Ahaz had a moment of silent awe. The meeting had likely been called by King Ahaz, and he received some comfort.

Another day, that message was added to: "For to us a child is born, to us a son is given, and the government will be on his shoulders. And he will be called Wonderful Counselor, Mighty God, Everlasting Father, Prince of Peace . . . He will reign on David's throne . . . from that time on and forever" (Isa. 9:6–7).

Chapter 11 of Isaiah also presents a special person:

A shoot will come up from the stump of Jesse; from his roots a Branch will bear fruit. The Spirit of the Lord will rest on him . . . The wolf will live with the lamb . . . and a little child will lead them . . . In that day the Root of Jesse will stand as a banner for the peoples; the nations will rally to him, and his resting place will be glorious . . . He will raise a banner for the nations . . . from the four quarters of the earth.

All people everywhere of all cultures are to listen to that and anticipate further explanation!

Destruction of surrounding nations is by plan: "Surely, as I have planned, so it will be, and as I have purposed, so it will happen . . . This is the plan determined for the whole world; this is the hand stretched out over all nations. For the Lord Almighty has purposed, and who can thwart him?" (Isa. 14:24–27). Look: "The realm of the dead below is all astir to meet you at your coming" (Isa. 14:9).

Hearken: "In love a throne will be established; in faithfulness a man will sit on it—one from the house of David—one who in judging seeks justice and speeds the cause of righteousness" (Isa. 16:5). Even the earth will receive judgment. When?

"On this mountain he will destroy the shroud that enfolds all peoples . . . he will swallow up death forever" (Isa. 25:7–8). Then it turns to praise:

"You will keep in perfect peace those whose minds are steadfast, because they trust in you" (Isa. 26:3). "But your dead will live, Lord; their bodies will rise" (Isa. 26:19). Others will worship the Lord on the holy mountain in Jerusalem. "Suddenly, in an instant, the Lord Almighty will come with thunder and earthquake and great noise, with windstorm and tempest and flames of a devouring fire" (Isa. 29:5–6). "See, a king will reign in righteousness" (Isa. 32:1). The Lord plans vengeance. There will be a "Way of Holiness" (Isa. 35:8) with only the redeemed sometime in the future. We do have assurance because of God's continuing love.

Chapter 40 introduces a new phase:

> Comfort, comfort my people, says your God. Speak tenderly to Jerusalem, and proclaim to her that her hard service has been completed, that her sin has been paid for, that she has received from the Lord's hand double for all her sins . . . Those who hope in the Lord will renew their strength. They will soar on wings like eagles; they will run and not grow weary, they will walk and not be faint. (Isa. 40:1–2, 31)

"My purpose will stand, and I will do all that I please" (Isa. 46:10). The extent of that comfort and intention implies a distant future.

The word *servant* has already appeared in the text, and Isaiah 41:8 and Isaiah 49:3 apply it to Israel. That is a large group of people.

However, notice the emotional progression that begins at chapter 48: "I foretold the former things long ago . . . From now on I will tell you new things, of hidden things unknown to you . . . Listen to me, Jacob, Israel, whom I have called: I am he; I am the first and I am the last. . . . Yes, I have called him. I will bring him, and he will succeed in his mission . . . Come near me and listen to this."

Chapter 49 continues the progression: "Listen to me, you islands; hear this, you distant nations . . . You are my servant, Israel, in whom I will display my splendor" (Isa. 49:1, 3). By means of Israel, something special will happen. "And now the Lord says" something different: "I will also make you a light for the Gentiles, that my salvation may reach to the ends of the earth . . . This is what the Lord says—the Redeemer and Holy One of Israel—to him who was despised and abhorred by the nation" (Isa. 49:5–7). That circumstance, we will observe later, occurs in Christ Jesus. "See, I will beckon to the nations . . . Then all mankind will know that I, the Lord, am your Savior, your Redeemer" (Isa. 49:22, 26). *Nations* and *mankind* mean the rest of humanity!

Note that the record states the "Holy One of Israel" (first mentioned in 5:19 and 5:24)—one person, not a group. This refers to Christ Jesus, as we will learn in the New Testament. Chapter 50 of Isaiah titles the Lord as "Sovereign."

Next are promises, beginning in chapter 51: "My salvation will last forever, my righteousness will never fail . . . My righteousness will last forever, my salvation through all generations . . . Awake, awake! . . . From that cup, the goblet of my wrath, you will never drink again." Salvation is for all generations!

Further, "Awake, awake, Zion . . . For the Lord has comforted his people, he has redeemed Jerusalem . . . See, my servant will act wisely; he will be raised and lifted up and highly exalted . . . For what they were not told, they will see, and what they have not heard, they will understand" (Isa. 52). Such indicates an individual, "the Holy One of [out of] Israel." The individual male Holy One is noted thirty times in Isaiah. Verses 13–15 of chapter 52 form a preface to chapter 53.

Only now are we ready to read chapter 53! Read it—every word of it—in your Bible at home. Then close your Bible and weep. Open it and read again the last sentence: "For he bore the sin of many, and made intercession for the transgressors" (Isa. 53:12). That's the extent of God's love. God paid, not you. That Holy One replaces the animal God first used! The contract of love is complete (for now).

This is for all nations, not just Israel! Remember—the covenant of love applies no matter what your behavior is! Cry out, "I need this One!" You cannot amend it or delete God's offer, but sadly, you can ignore it.

About a dozen features detailed in chapter 53 are identical to the crucifixion of Christ Jesus! This is the gospel of the Old Testament. *Gospel* means "good news"—sins as white as snow (Isa. 1:18). Indeed! God's will is expressed by love and events!

We find this wonderful promise slipped within these declarations: "My thoughts are not your thoughts, neither are your ways my ways . . . My word . . . will accomplish what I desire and achieve the purpose for which I sent it" (Isa. 55:8, 11).

There is more to be revealed: "See, I will create new heavens and a new earth. The former things will not be remembered" (Isa. 65:17–24). The contrast of accepting this One or not is stark, as pictured by the closing words: "As the new heavens and the new earth that I make will endure before me, . . . all mankind will come and bow down before me . . . And they will go out and look on the dead bodies of those who rebelled against me; the worms that eat them will not die; the fire that burns them will not be quenched, and they will be loathsome to all mankind" (Isa. 66:22–24). All this was revealed to Isaiah and recorded six or seven centuries before Christ Jesus came!

You and I are born in God's love. Love continued with promises, over and over! The ball is in your court! What is your response?

FROM JEREMIAH

The word of the Lord came to Jeremiah, and he received visions, different yet dramatic. "Declares the Lord" is stated more than 150 times in the book of Jeremiah. The ancient Hebrew texts are quite different from the ancient Greek texts. The history in Jeremiah leads to the exile. Before reading the text, we must be alerted to repetition, used to elicit attention. Watch for the use of these words: Almighty, anger, completely, covenant, declares, destroy, disaster, forsaken, listen, name, nations, north, remnant, restore, return, vengeance, and wrath.

Jeremiah received a direct commission: "Before I formed you in the womb I knew you, before you were born I set you apart; I appointed you as a prophet to the nations . . . Do not be afraid of them, for I am with you and will rescue you" (Jer. 1:5, 8).

The first message is that disaster will come upon Jerusalem from the north because they had forsaken the Lord, had burned incense to other gods, and exhibited no awe of the Lord their God. Notice the depth of their excuse: "It's no use. I love foreign gods, and I must go after them" (Jer. 2:25). The Lord's plea to them is clear. He urges them to acknowledge Him and return, "for I am your husband" (Jer. 3:14). Also, "At that time they will call Jerusalem The Throne of the Lord, and all nations will gather in Jerusalem to honor the name of the Lord" (Jer. 3:17). "How gladly would I treat you like my children" (Jer. 3:19).

"Return" is emphasized (thirty-one times, including seven times in chapter 3). Destruction is described: "If you can find but one person who deals honestly and seeks the truth, I will forgive this city . . . Yet even in those days . . . I will not destroy you completely" (Jer. 5:1, 18). The critique of the people continues chapter after chapter. The Lord often injects his urgent invitation of love. Occasionally the Lord indicates his future plan: "But after I uproot them, I will again have compassion and will bring each of them back to their own inheritance and their own country . . . But if any nation does not listen, I will completely uproot and destroy it" (Jer. 12:15–17). God so loves that he tells about the future.

Aha! Here is the "heart" of the human problem: "The heart is deceitful above all things and beyond cure" (Jer. 17:9). That is the Lord's judgment, whether we agree or not. What will help? "It's no use. We will continue with our own plans; we will all follow the stubbornness of our evil hearts" (Jer. 18:12). One of the Lord's monikers for the people of Israel is "stiff-necked." That reminds us that the problem began with Adam and Eve and the people were cautioned years later to "Love the Lord your God with all your heart and with all your soul and with all your strength" (Deut. 6:5). Reading further, we will learn that the Holy Spirit repairs our hearts, and still later, a new body will replace our hearts (souls).

Portions of Jeremiah are in poetic lines. Jerusalem is named forty times in the first eighteen chapters. Jeremiah struggled with his emotions.

Now we have a promise: "I will raise up for David a righteous Branch, a King who will reign wisely . . . The Lord Our Righteous Savior" (Jer. 23:5–6).

The Lord will use the king of Babylon, Nebuchadnezzar, to serve him. Judah will be there in Babylon, in captivity for seventy years! God does not show favoritism, but justice.

The dramatic figure of speech of the "cup of God's wrath" is recorded in chapter 25 three times. Don't misunderstand *relent*; that is not a cancellation, but is only a delay of judgment. The king of Judah is addressed several times. Jeremiah was threatened with death, but was spared.

The Lord does not forget: "When seventy years are completed for Babylon, I will come to you and fulfill my good promise to bring you back to this place. For I know the plans I have for you . . . to prosper you and . . . to give you hope and a future" (Jer. 29:10–11). The returning and future details are given in chapters 29–31. God, in love, reveals.

The Lord had commissioned Jeremiah, allowed many disasters, and protected him. The book of Jeremiah presents detailed critiques of nations, including Egypt, Philistia, Moab, Ammon, Edom, Damascus, Babylon (at length), and others. Jeremiah passed on what the Lord declared. Judah's judgment was exile to Babylon.

Books have been written containing the comforting promises found in the book of Jeremiah. Notice also the many discomforting promises. God made us to be lovers. All these judgments are based upon the obvious lack of love for God, as the people did not even acknowledge God's sovereignty.

Isaiah urged the people to listen, but Jeremiah critiqued them because they did not listen.

FROM LAMENTATIONS

Presumably, Jeremiah wrote this. The printed form in English indicates it was written in Hebrew poetic form.

While in exile, those remaining in Jerusalem expressed their emotions: "Look, Lord, on my affliction, for the enemy has triumphed" (Lam. 1:9) There was a struggle for food. Emotions became grievous. They recognized that all of this was the result of God's judgment. They somewhat anticipated this, and now they had to live it. "The Lord has done what he planned" (Lam. 2:17).

They also had trust in God: "Because of the Lord's great love we are not consumed, for his compassions never fail . . . It is good to wait quietly for the salvation of the Lord . . . Though he brings grief, he will show compassion, so great is his unfailing love . . . Is it not from the mouth of the Most High that both calamities and good things come? Why should the living complain when punished for their sins?" (Lam. 3:22, 26, 32, 38–39). And near the end of the book: "You, Lord, reign forever; your throne endures from generation to generation" (Lam. 5:19).

God's sovereignty includes unfailing love!

FROM EZEKIEL

Be alert if you are reading from the NIV. It presents the title *sovereign* over two hundred times in Ezekiel! That is from the Hebrew and is a beautiful emphasis for us. Instead of "Lord God," we now have "Sovereign Lord." Also, the translators used *therefore* at least sixty times. Understand that Ezekiel's words following the *therefore* present a consequence that logically and even necessarily follow the words just preceding the *therefore*. Ezekiel is intentional. (The first use of *therefore* is in Ezekiel 5:7.)

It appears that a scribe recorded Ezekiel's authority: "The hand of the Lord was on him" (Ezek. 1:3), as he asserts later (Ezek. 3:22). Strange mechanisms or creatures seemed to represent awesomeness and the unexplainable. Then a voice told of difficulty. Along with the godly assignment was the significant title *Son of Man* (used in Ezekiel maybe a hundred times). Ezekiel presents him as a reliable spokesman for God. Daniel later presents the Son of Man as equal to God, and still later we will observe that Christ Jesus himself claims that title.

"This is Jerusalem, which I have set in the center of the nations, with countries all around her" (Ezek. 5:5). That reminds us that Moses recorded the fact that these folks were chosen to represent God on earth as sons of God (Ex. 4:22). However, because of their wickedness, God would be against them and there would be doom and disaster. The Spirit, by visions, took Ezekiel to Jerusalem where he saw detestable—yes, detestable—conduct by the elders. Some were killed. They were conforming to the neighboring nations! Even so, God's love is unfailing. For example, God says, "I will give them an undivided heart and put a new spirit in them; I will remove from them their heart of stone and give them a heart of flesh. Then they will follow my decrees and be careful to keep my laws. They will be my people, and I will be their God" (Ezek. 11:19–20). In the meantime, they would go into exile. Judgment often has three features: sword, famine, and plague.

God's love extends beyond earthly judgments: "I will establish my covenant with you, and you will know that I am the Lord. Then, when I make atonement for you for all you have done, you will remember" (Ezek. 16:62–63). God already provided the life of an animal for Adam and Eve. God will provide the permanent atonement! When? How?

After a discussion of death, we are told, "For I take no pleasure in the death of anyone, declares the Sovereign Lord. Repent and live!" (Ezek. 18:32). This is repeated two more times in the book of Ezekiel.

Chapter 20 is a thorough historical review of why the people are without excuse, and it ends with one of the saddest sentences of the Book: "Isn't he just telling parables?" (Ezek. 20:49).

"I tried to cleanse you but you would not be cleansed . . . The time has come for me to act. I will not hold back; I will not have pity, nor will I relent" (Ezek. 24:13–14). Exile is covered in several chapters. "I am going to do these things, but for the sake of my holy name, which you have profaned" (Ezek. 36:22). God's unfailing love continues, though, as *rescue* and *return* are expressed several times. There will be one nation. "For though I sent them into exile among the nations, I will gather them to their own land . . . for I will pour out my Spirit on the people of Israel" (Ezek. 39:28–29).

Ezekiel was told to pass on to others all that he saw (chapters 40–43). There would be a new temple in which "I will live among them forever" (Ezek. 43:9). Then more directly, the Lord spoke to Ezekiel as though someone important was to be introduced—and the prince was introduced. Many believe that chapters 44–47 are foretelling that the prince is Christ Jesus, who will return. The city established will be given the name "THE LORD IS THERE" (Ezek. 48:35). All this is yet in our future, by God's unfailing love!

FROM DANIEL

Daniel and three friends were taken with many others into exile in Babylon. These four were selected and prepared to enter the king's service.

Shortly thereafter, king Nebuchadnezzar had a dream, and of course he wanted it interpreted. He demanded to be told the dream and also its meaning! Stalemate! There was no answer. The immediate decree was that the wise men were to be killed. As Daniel and his friends pleaded to God for his mercy, God gave Daniel a vision of a huge statue whose portions were of various materials. The portions represented four successive kingdoms, of which Nebuchadnezzar was the head or the first. The rock that smashed it would be a creation of God, not at all human in origin. Daniel praised God for the revelation and explained it to the king, emphasizing that the rock represented a kingdom that would be established by God that will never end. (The reference to a mountain is likely Mt. Zion.) Even the king had praise: "Surely your God is the God of gods and the Lord of kings and a revealer of mysteries" (Dan. 2:47).

The king's pride obviously rose as he built a gold image ninety feet tall with the command that all people of every culture must fall and worship it or they would be thrown into a blazing furnace. The quick observation was that these four Jews in high position did not worship the golden image. The king called the three friends to account. Here is their beautiful, loving confidence in the loving God: "The God we serve is able to deliver us from it [the blazing furnace], and he will deliver us from Your Majesty's hand. But even if he does not, we want you to know, Your Majesty, that we will not serve your gods or worship the image of gold you have set up" (Dan. 3:17–18).

In the furnace, the first evidence of God's hand was that the king saw four men walking about, and one was like a god. The king instructed them to step out, which they did—with no evidence of having been in the furnace. That was a second evidence of God's hand. The king credited an angel for the protection and praised them: "They trusted in him [their God] and defied the king's command and were willing to give up their lives rather than serve or worship any god except their own God" (Dan. 3:28). Nebuchadnezzar added that any countryman who spoke against this God would be destroyed. Very systematically, he told his people that God's kingdom "is an eternal kingdom; his dominion endures from generation to generation" (Dan. 4:3).

The king had another dream, a very strange one, and of course he called for Daniel, who had "the spirit of the holy gods" (Dan. 4:18). Daniel politely explained that the message pertained to the king personally. In the midst of the king's success and grandeur, he would be reduced to an animal's life until he acknowledged "that the Most High is sovereign over all kingdoms on earth and gives them to anyone he wishes" (Dan. 4:25). Also, his kingdom would be restored. With politeness, Daniel said, "Renounce your sins by doing what is right, and your wickedness by being kind to the oppressed" (Dan. 4:27).

A year later, as the king praised himself, a voice declared the application of the earlier dream. Immediately Nebuchadnezzar was like one of the cattle and was eating grass. Sure enough, at the end of seven years his sanity was restored and his testimony apparently was from his heart, praising the Most High: "Now I, Nebuchadnezzar, praise and exalt and glorify the King of heaven, because everything he does is right and all his ways are just. And those who walk in pride he is able to humble" (Dan. 4:37).

The next king, Belshazzar, gave a grand banquet and praised material gods. A hand appeared and wrote on the wall, terrifying everyone at the banquet. When Daniel was called, he reviewed the entire experience of the king's father and explained the writing as meaning the end of Belshazzar's days of rule, the inadequacy of Belshazzar's life, and Belshazzar's kingdom being given to the Medes and Persians. That very night the change took place!

The new local administrators could not fault Daniel, and so they contrived with the king, Darius, that anyone who prayed to any god other than to Darius during the next thirty days would be thrown to the lions. Daniel continued to pray almost conspicuously three times a day. Upon this being reported, the king was grieved. The decree stands! As Daniel was thrown to the lions, the king told him, "May your God, whom you serve continually, rescue you!" (Dan. 6:16).

The king had an emotional, sleepless night. At dawn he called out, "Daniel, servant of the living God, has your God, whom you serve continually, been able to rescue you from the lions?" (Dan. 6:20).

Daniel replied, "May the king live forever! My God sent his angel, and he shut the mouths of the lions. They have not hurt me, because I was found innocent in his sight" (Dan. 6:21–22). No wound was found in Daniel's flesh. The contriving leaders and families died at the "hands" of the lions. The king decreed, "In every part of my kingdom people must fear and reverence the God of Daniel" (Dan. 6:26). Daniel prospered during the reign of that king and the next.

Now we see a distinct change in the text. The dreams are Daniel's rather than the king's. Notice that "Most High" is used fourteen times. It is a title likely to have attracted the attention of the non-Hebrew people. Daniel had identified "Most High" with the sovereign Lord (Dan. 5:21).

We are told that approximately the first half of Daniel was written in Aramaic, perhaps so that the non-Hebrew people could readily read it. Also, that was the language Daniel was using. There are many critics of portions of the book of Daniel. This book you are reading is emphasizing that the Holy Spirit guided the early Christian leaders to provide us with a very adequate text to be used down through the centuries. Jesus referred to the writing of Daniel (Matt. 24:15). Much of the kingship mentioned in Daniel thus far can be verified by civil literature.

Many books have been written about the events in these next chapters. "One like a son of man" will arrive from the sky and will establish a kingdom for all people (Dan. 7:13–14). He will act as God! In contrast, a human kingdom will exist and will oppress the saints for three and a half years. The human kingdom will be completely destroyed—forever. Let's give Satan (though not mentioned) credit for arranging the above human opposition.

In the midst of all this, "We do not make requests of you because we are righteous, but because of your great mercy. Lord, listen! Lord, forgive! Lord, hear and act! For your sake, my God, do not delay, because your city and your people bear your Name" (Dan. 9:18–19). "There will be a time of distress . . . Everyone whose name is found written in the book—will be delivered. Multitudes who sleep in the dust of the earth will awake: some to everlasting life, others to shame and everlasting contempt" (Dan. 12:1–2). "Seal the words" (Dan. 12:4).

Some leaders today believe they have this all meticulously calculated. Simply said, there will be lengthy times of unimaginable conflict. God is sovereign! There will be one of two outcomes for each person: everlasting life or everlasting contempt.

FROM HOSEA TO ZEPHANIAH:

HOSEA, JOEL, AMOS, OBADIAH, JONAH, MICAH, NAHUM, HABAKKUK, ZEPHANIAH

These and the next three books are called the Minor Prophets simply because they are much shorter than the previous prophetic books. These first nine of the twelve books can be grouped together by subject since they record time prior to the captivity or within the exile. Most can be assigned dates by the named kings of their time and by secular history. Some of these prophets warned the Northern Kingdom (Israel), some warned the Southern Kingdom (Judah), and some warned the neighboring nations. Some of those who recorded the words of the prophets likely met others who were doing the same.

Hosea records announcements of impending disaster so vivid and depressing. A few sentences into the pages we have encouragement: "I will say to those called 'Not my people,' 'You are my people,' and they will say, 'You are my God'" (Hos. 2:23). Also, "You will call me 'my husband'" (Hos. 2:16). Hosea was told to love the people as God loves them, despite wrong worship. Further, "I long to redeem them . . . They do not cry out to me from their hearts . . . They do not turn to the Most High" (Hos. 7:13–16). In the distant future, "I will deliver this people from the power of the grave; I will redeem them from death. Where, O death, are your plagues? Where, O grave, is your destruction?" (Hos. 13:14). Many pages later in the Book we will see the apostle Paul using this taunt (1 Cor. 15:55).

Joel tells of destruction by locusts and also of a distant future—sometime: "I will pour out my Spirit on all people. Your sons and daughters will prophesy . . . I will show wonders in the heavens and on the earth . . . before the coming of the great and dreadful day of the Lord. And everyone who calls on the name of the Lord will be saved" (Joel 2:28–32).

A reader asks God,
> "Me, of a distant nation, loved by you, Lord God?"
> "Yes, you."
> "Me!"

Amos details disasters. "Surely the Sovereign Lord does nothing without revealing his plan to his servants the prophets" (Amos 3:7). Yet God says that sometime in their future, "I will plant Israel in their own land, never again to be uprooted from the land I have given them" (Amos 9:15). Apparently that took place in 1948!

Obadiah stresses that God's judgmental destruction will come upon all nations. The Hebrew folk will center upon Mt. Zion: "And the kingdom will be the Lord's" (verse 21).

For **Jonah**, let's start with a touch of drama by using an illustration. Someone in our society jumps at the opportunity to chide us believers. Let's listen: "Hey, Jonah, you said you were swallowed by a whale and regurgitated onto the shore alive and well! I have difficulty not laughing. You should have joined the local liar's club. You would have won the next contest, hands down."

The premise above is also the premise of many in our society who believe that God has not produced miracles. They may not have been as forthright as the illustration shows, but deep down, many cling to that premise. One response is to ask such people to read the Book all the way through from page one and then arrive at a conclusion. However, the tour de force is Jesus's specific reference (recorded twice: Matthew 12:39–40 and Luke 11:29–30) to Jonah's actual experience! For someone who is sincerely inquiring, the answer is, "You'd like to know how, but don't need to know." A miracle of God stands. Our reading from the Book has already imbedded many miracles into our confidence. Many of those are validated by known history.

Now back to Jonah's text. Jonah is another example of the fickleness of human nature. Apparently he had no love for Nineveh. He ran. Some consider this to be merely a parable. Jesus referred to it without qualification. After being rescued from a special fish God provided, Jonah did preach at Nineveh. "The Ninevites believed God" (Jonah 3:5). History records that destruction occurred years later.

Micah presents a different feature besides physical disaster: "Therefore night will come over you, without visions, and darkness, without divination. The sun will set for the prophets, and the day will go dark for them . . . because there is no answer from God" (Mic. 3:6–7). That appears to be foretelling the four hundred years between the Old Testament and New Testament writings!

Almost in fine print that can be so easily missed in the midst of major topics is, "But you, Bethlehem Ephrathah, though you are small among the clans of Judah, out of you will come for me one who will be ruler over Israel, whose origins are from of old, from ancient times" (Mic. 5:2). We await the record of the wise men's visit to Mary and Joseph.

The Lord expects justice, mercy, and humility in walking with God (Mic. 6:8).

Nahum says Nineveh will be destroyed. Apparently the people did very little changing of worship after Jonah left. In contrast, the splendor of Jacob will be restored.

Habakkuk helps our impatience as we wait and watch. Any time we tend to think God does not mean what he says, we need to read the Lord's response:

Write down the revelation and make it plain . . . For the revelation awaits an appointed time; it speaks of the end and will not prove false. Though it linger, wait for it; it will certainly come and will not delay

. . . but the righteous person will live by his faithfulness . . . For the earth will be filled with the knowledge of the glory of the Lord . . . The Lord is in his holy temple; let all the earth be silent before him. (Hab. 2:2–4, 14, 20)

Living by faith was stressed by the apostle Paul (Gal. 3:11). Habakkuk includes a beautiful closing prayer about waiting patiently, even for the day of calamity.

Zephaniah declared, "Be silent before the Sovereign Lord, for the day of the Lord is near. The Lord has prepared a sacrifice; he has consecrated those he has invited" (Zeph. 1:7). When will we see it? Chapter 1 tells of a special day fourteen times in reference to judgment. "The Lord your God is with you, the Mighty Warrior who saves. He will take great delight in you; in his love he will no longer rebuke you, but will rejoice over you with singing" (Zeph. 3:17). In the midst of repeated declarations of disaster, some by nature and some by warfare, we have God's love evident time after time as he promises to gather and restore the Hebrew people, and even gentile nations. "I will give you honor and praise among all the peoples of the earth when I restore your fortunes before your very eyes" (Zeph. 3:20).

FROM HAGGAI, ZECHARIAH, AND MALACHI

These three books record activity of those who returned from exile. Some gentile leaders hindered them, and some kings encouraged their rebuilding.

Haggai gave the Lord's criticism that they were attentive to building their houses instead of rebuilding the temple. They took heed from Haggai and began rebuilding the temple. "From this day on I will bless you" (Hag. 2:19). "On that day . . . I will make you like my signet ring, for I have chosen you" (Hag. 2:23). You were born in God's love. Despite also being born with a self-as-god nature, God continues with unfailing love! As one who cries for restoration to peace with God, the response is that you are as a mark, as a gem, on God's ring of love.

Zechariah recorded repentance: "The Lord Almighty has done to us what our ways and practices deserve, just as he determined to do" (Zech. 1:6). He received several messages from angels or visions. "Shout and be glad, Daughter Zion. For I am coming, and I will live among you . . . I will live among you and you will know that the Lord Almighty has sent me to you . . . Be still before the Lord, all mankind, because he has roused himself from his holy dwelling" (Zech. 2:10–13). "I am going to bring my servant, the Branch" (Zech. 3:8). "[He will] build the temple of the Lord . . . and he will be clothed with majesty and will sit and rule on his throne" (Zech. 6:12–13). "Not by might nor by power, but by my Spirit . . . Then he will bring out the capstone to shouts of 'God bless it! God bless it!'" (Zech. 4:6–7). "I will return to Zion and dwell in Jerusalem. Then Jerusalem will be called the Faithful City . . . [on] the Holy Mountain . . . I will save my people from the countries of the east and the west. I will bring them back to live in Jerusalem; they will be my people" (Zech. 8:3, 7–8).

"Rejoice greatly, Daughter Zion! Shout, Daughter Jerusalem! See, your king comes to you, righteous and victorious, lowly and riding on a donkey" (Zech. 9:9). A king on a beast of burden? Yes! Behold, Christ Jesus did just that! Also, the Lord will protect Jerusalem from the nations that attack. Chapter 12 contains these promises: "I will make Jerusalem an immovable rock for all the nations . . . On that day I will set out to destroy all the nations that attack Jerusalem. And I will pour out on the house of David and the inhabitants of Jerusalem a spirit of grace and supplication" (Zech. 12:3, 9–10). Hearken to a future duet: "I will say, 'They are my people,' and they will say, 'The Lord is our God'" (Zech. 13:9).

There will be a unique time entitled "that day" (mentioned twelve times in chapter 14), which will include days of joy rather than remorse. Among the promises, we read:

I will gather all the nations to Jerusalem . . . On that day [the Lord's] feet will stand on the Mount of Olives . . . Then the Lord my God will come, and all the holy ones with him . . . There will be . . . no distinction between day and night . . . On that day living water will flow out from Jerusalem . . . The Lord will be king over the whole earth. On that day there will be one Lord, and his name the only name . . . The survivors . . . will go up year after year to worship the King, the Lord Almighty. (Zech. 14)

Let's read Zechariah 14:9 again: "The Lord will be king over the whole earth."

Malachi appears to be anticlimactic after the previous book. God gave Malachi the subject that was to challenge the level of response of the people. God seems to refine Hebrew thinking by wording questions for them or wording what they should be asking. The answers have been given time and again. It is they who have become careless, not God. Nevertheless, God will even send a messenger ahead of the return of the Lord. "And you will again see the distinction between the righteous and the wicked, between those who serve God and those who do not" (Mal. 3:18). We see that God's plan for the future is intact; it is the individual's plan that is dubious.

Many, many promises were made. Many have not yet been fulfilled.

You have now gone through three-quarters of the Book. I hope you are learning to learn by using the whole context—your Bible—in your natural language. What is your response? Are you weeping in repentance, shouting for joy, or bowing in silent awe?

Remember—of all the God-created things (list your favorites), does God talk to them? Can they talk to God? God only made one creature for communication and able to recognize love—people! You are one of these!

With this one Book—the Bible—in hand, we have read a few hundred pages that span many, many, centuries. Give the Holy Spirit credit as editor in chief for guiding people to choose which experiences to include and which ones to leave out of the text. Obviously, no human committee could create this. God has inspired—breathed out—his will.

Your Book, the Bible, is God's love letter!

BLACKOUT?

A TIME FOR PATIENCE

ONE CENTURY PASSED. A second century passed. A third century passed. Even a fourth went by—in silence. No new prophets had come on the scene since the last writing of the prophets. How many generations was that?

We would be impressed by this if our Bibles had four blank pages between the Old and New Testaments to represent those four centuries. Yes, other books and letters were written that were not selected for the biblical canon.

Let's offer an illustration. A grand fireworks presentation ends with hundreds of colorful rockets almost simultaneously. Then suddenly—blackout! A casual comparison is that the multitude of these minor prophets, which followed the major prophets, were a grand display by God. Then suddenly—blackout! However, you remember what you recently read in the Book—what you read in the previous pages.

During this intertestamental period (the period between the Old and New Testaments), what rejoicing or lament did these people have? Some may have shaken their fists at God. Much more importantly during this time of silence, how many touches of God's love were counted by contemplating the past centuries? Hopefully, many turned to their Bibles (scrolls). Hopefully, many read from Genesis through Deuteronomy and also the other books as they were written and added.

The people of this modern age find it hard to understand the difficulty of preparing the writing material back then, which involved slow, tedious hand copying, and even the slow transporting of the writings from village to village. The priests had the written messages, but the populace did not. Soon we will read Abraham's words (from Jesus's parable) given as a reprimand: "They have Moses and the Prophets; let them listen to them" (Luke 16:29). The Jews protected the scrolls in the temple. Humanity had the lesson from Job urging them to cry for an advocate.

The Greeks then ruled, and their language had become the common one, which was an advantage to everyone. Very significantly, sometime in the third century BC, the Hebrew Bible (at least the first five books) was translated into Greek. Tradition notes that seventy men did this; hence the name "Septuagint."

In the second century BC, a Hebrew family with the nickname of Maccabee began a revolt against civil rule, and they did well for a few decades. Roman rule was growing. Roads were built and some were surfaced, eliminating mud. Ship building was growing. In summary, communication and trade were at a new level.

Blackout? Not exactly. Instead, the curtains were closed for some time, ready to open with something new! Let us peek into the New Testament: "But when the set time had fully come, God sent his Son, born of a woman" (Gal. 4:4).

Let's consider a few things to help us carry onward with assurance and with high expectation:

- God is Lord and sovereign. There is one God. God is not whimsical, incidental, or accidental, but is consistent and intentional. His love is evident in all activity.
- God created us as lovers. Each one of us is born into that love.
- God gave the first, though temporary, life-for-life substitution for our needed change of heart from self-as-god, which we inherited from Adam and Eve.

- God is righteous in choosing a level of separation to illustrate the result of freewill choice to live as self-as-god, and hence to live separately from God's rule.

- God has intervened many times in diverse ways to show his glory.

- God has clearly assured people of every island and nation of his desire for their presence in the future. In the meantime, we rejoice in being born in God's love, despite our conduct.

- God has assured us that a special person will arrive on earth. That person needs to be human, yet vastly superior in order to properly represent both people and God. That one has been named the Rock, Branch, Anointed One, King, Advocate, Redeemer, Son of Man, and Bearer of our Iniquities (including my iniquity). *Iniquity* here means that we are not equal to what Adam and Eve were originally. We now have the inner self prone to act as one's own god.

- God has allowed a detractor, Satan, to continue to exist within sovereign bounds, but who is under contract to be eliminated.

- God encourages us to multiply, even though each person is born with an inner nature of self-as-god, which we cannot reform. We are in desperate need of a plan from God.

- God made promises not only for that correction, but also for many special events, and even for a future that will include a righteous ruler and God's personal presence. The detractor cannot delete those promises! God has sovereign control over what he allows.

The consistency and progressiveness of all things in the Book implies that there has been one editor in chief throughout those centuries, resulting in the parts forming an integral whole. The Book is not a diary of a multitude of events, but it is a selective recording of significant events that lead to purposes. That is not surprising, for writing these things down at that time and copying them was costly and tedious. Any future writing showing that God's promises have been kept (fulfilled) will authenticate the previous writings.

Let's try a definition of life on earth using ordinary words. God places each person here to recognize and cherish his love. This earth-life is a test program. It is not difficult, for we have been given an inner desire to continue in some fashion after this earth-life. God's love rewards us when we desire to please God. After our earthly death we will be raised and asked for the final time, "Do you love God?" Either answer will be met with an appropriate finality. God has prepared the contract and signed it, handing it to every individual to believe or not. We will be able to be more specific as we continue to read the Book.

The Book has given us history, biographies of three personalities, and numerous revelations that we could not possibly concoct on our own with any veracity. The Book is our answering service. Yes, there are many matters I would like to know, yet don't need to understand. I find that the Book tells me God's view of what I need to know. How gracious of God to give us assurance!

Please finish reading all of what is labeled the Old Testament in your Bible in order to be ready for the next section. Will we find that the newer material is a replacement of the older material or that it is very relative to the older material? Many books have been written noting the carefulness and time involved in the formation of both the Old and the New Testaments.

The world's theater had not turned black; the lights had only dimmed. The world was left in high suspense, ready for the curtain to open upon a grand display. So let's proceed with those high expectations of what else God wants you, the reader, to understand! Ask the Spirit of God to guide and thrill you.

Your Bible is . . .

    a selective history Book,

    a community answering service, and

    a personal letter of love.

MATTHEW TO ACTS OF THE APOSTLES

FROM MATTHEW

MATTHEW OPENS WITH A CLAIM that this will be a record of "Christ" (*Christ* is a Greek word). The NIV uses "Messiah" (*Messiah* is a Hebrew word). Both *Christ* and *Messiah* in their original languages mean "anointed one." "Anointed One" elicits thoughts of a king, priest, or prophet. Matthew as an apostle was an eyewitness of Jesus's words and actions. He had been a tax collector and so was skilled in record keeping. We will find that he gives many more references to the Old Testament than any other writer. We need to read!

The genealogy in the Gospel of Matthew begins with Abraham, includes David, and ends with Christ. The name of Abraham grabs the attention of Hebrew folk who rate a person by heritage rather than wealth. *Abraham* also enlivens the attention of any reader to the entire Old Testament. Everything that follows is intended to enhance what has already been claimed.

Next comes a quandary for a man named Joseph, who is told by his fiancée that she is with child by the Holy Spirit instead of by man! Why should he believe that? *Thank you, Lord, for sending an angel who affirmed that Mary was to be his wife and that the child was to be given the name "Jesus" because he would save people from their sins.* A variant of the name, Joshua, had been prominent long before, but that earlier Jesus (Joshua) did not save anyone from sin.

Matthew referred to what had been given to Isaiah centuries ago (Matt. 1:23, quoted from Isa. 7:14): "'The virgin will conceive and give birth to a son, and they will call him Immanuel' (which means 'God with us')." That is what Solomon had pondered at the dedication of the temple! For Joseph and Mary, ordinary citizens, those are two big pills to swallow. Seriously, Joseph was patiently compliant. This Jesus, birthed by God the Creator-Father, was commissioned before birth—before he had done anything!

Heads up! Some men following a star (a special light God created for a particular purpose) arrived and asked Herod, the ruler, about a child who would become king! God had communicated to men who used astronomy. Talking to a ruler about his replacement is a good way to lose one's head. Of course that disturbed Herod, who managed to have enough poise to ask for a Scripture review. "Bethlehem . . . out of you will come a ruler who will shepherd my people Israel" (Matt. 2:6, quoted from Mic. 5:2). The ruler concealed his fury. The visitors found and worshiped the infant Jesus and were directed homeward in safety. An angel directed the family, with the wealth of their presents, to flee to Egypt.

Later, the ruler let out his fury by killing infants in the region. Upon his death, the family was directed to return, and thus another promise took place, or was fulfilled: "Out of Egypt I called my son" (Matt. 2:15, quoted from Hos. 11:1). God directed the parents of the child in order to allow him to live in safety.

Several years later in the countryside, a strange fellow named John proclaimed, "Repent, for the kingdom of heaven has come near" (Matt. 3:2). After four hundred years, that was a startling message, and people flocked to hear and were baptized in the Jordan River. From then on, this man was known as John the Baptist. One day he called attention to a person who would have something to do with the Holy Spirit and fire. (*Holy One* was recorded many times by the prophets; however, *Holy Spirit* was a new title presented by the angel to Joseph and repeated by John the Baptist.)

Jesus came for baptism, too; however, as he came up out of the water, a voice from heaven declared, "This is my Son, whom I love; with him I am well pleased" (Matt. 3:17). That's an anointing by God! That's God's imprimatur upon Jesus. As God's (firstborn) Son, will he do better than the Israelites who had been so charged as God's representative (Ex. 4:22)? We anticipate that much evidence will be presented to show just that.

The 1984 edition of the New International Version retained the Greek word *son* (Matt. 5:9, 45), which hints at the specific responsible role of representing God, as previously referenced for the Israelites (Ex. 4:22). The 2011 edition of the NIV uses the word *children*. That relieves the fretting of some people over the implication that "son of God" is a specific gender for a believer, when it is not.

In a lonely place for forty days, Jesus was accosted by the devil, who tempted (suggested or urged him to do wrong) Jesus three times to give allegiance to him and worship him! Jesus's response was crucial: "Worship the Lord your God, and serve him only" (Matt. 4:10). Note that Jesus answered from Moses's record (Deut. 6:13).

Jesus began preaching publicly: "Repent, for the kingdom of heaven has come near" (Matt. 4:17). He called Peter and his brother Andrew to leave fishing, follow him, and become fishers of men. They did. In Galilee and in a large surrounding region, Jesus gave good news of the kingdom. Crowds followed—even ill people. He was preaching (thus far no content was recorded) and healing a variety of diseases. He did not promote a promise of healing everyone. How gracious that in the midst of preaching he presented his authority and love to so many by healing!

Suddenly Mathew records Jesus's subjects (chapters 5–7). Jesus dismissed the thought of a civil kingdom by blessing people of humble characteristics, saying, "Theirs is the kingdom of heaven" (Matt. 5:3). No reference to a civil kingdom is given! Daily lifestyle is desirable as salt and light so that others will praise "your Father in heaven" (Matt. 5:16). One's lifestyle and righteousness should surpass that of the religious leaders in order to enter the kingdom of heaven (Matt. 5:20). At least a dozen times, Jesus used the caution "but I tell you" to critique the inner attitude that precedes outward acts. For most of us, the most difficult expectation is, "But I tell you, love your enemies and pray for those who persecute you, that you may be children of your Father in heaven" (Matt. 5:44–45). Love helps replace hate. Pray in secret to your unseen Father, for "Your Father knows what you need before you ask him" (Matt. 6:8). Lay up treasures in heaven where there is no deterioration. "But seek first his kingdom and his righteousness, and all these things will be given to you as well" (Matt. 6:33). Persevere in asking, seeking, and knocking, and there will be answers. Such a lifestyle is likened to a narrow gateway. Only a few find it. The crowd's reaction to Jesus was one of amazement at his teaching and authority (Matt. 7:28–29).

From the lips of Jesus we learn what God expects of us today. God, who does not change, had expected people to live prior to the flood in the same way as this current teaching from Jesus. The flood record does not list that prior godly behavior. Apparently they were busy with their own self-as-god attitude!

Many times Jesus referred to God as "your Father," and when he spoke about himself, he referred to God as "my Father." It is no surprise, then, that Jesus's prayer recommends for us to use "our Father" (Matt. 6:9). We will watch for the explanation of his kingdom.

Jesus healed a leprous man, healed the servant of a Roman officer, cast out demons by giving a word, and calmed a storm. That's being sovereign! Those are gifts of love.

Upon healing a paralytic, Jesus added, "Take heart, son; your sins are forgiven" (Matt. 9:2). That spiked a reaction, for he, a man, claimed God's prerogative. Jesus had titled himself the "Son of Man," apparently referring to the God-man described in Daniel 7:13–14. Jesus had already demonstrated that he was, and is, God over this life and nature. To forgive sin is no surprise. He likened spiritual healing to medical healing; thus, he came for the "sick"—the sinners.

Jesus sent out his twelve disciples with authority over disease and demons.

On the one hand, Jesus taught that we should be afraid of our bodies and souls being destroyed in hell (Matt. 10:28; the context is the day of judgment), yet on the other hand he taught that we are worth more than many sparrows. Jesus warned, "Whoever acknowledges me before others, I will also acknowledge before my Father in heaven. But whoever disowns me before others, I will disown before my Father in heaven" (Matt. 10:32–33). Can we be sure?

Jesus constantly showed his unfailing love. "Come to me, all you who are weary and burdened, and I will give you rest. Take my yoke upon you and learn from me . . . For my yoke is easy and my burden is light" (Matt. 11:28–30). God loves us! A yoke is a means to carry a burden, not to avoid it.

Clearly speaking about himself, Jesus said, "The Son of Man will be three days and three nights in the heart of the earth" (Matt. 12:40). How could that come about?

Jesus asked the people to do the will of his Father in heaven. We know the basic answer to that is to "Love the Lord your God with all your heart and with all your soul and with all your mind" (Matt. 22:37). That, again, was intended to be the rule for living prior to the flood. Apparently it was ignored.

Two thoughts are common from the several parables of the kingdom of heaven. The first thought is that heaven is very desirable. The second is that there must be intention to obtain it. Jesus's loving attention to daily matters is illustrated by the next miracles of feeding more than five thousand people, walking on water, and feeding more than four thousand people. The relationship with Jesus is from one's heart. The attitude of the heart precedes behavior.

Religious leaders twice asked Jesus to perform a sign for them. Both times he answered by referring to Jonah, who had been "entombed" and then brought back to "life" ashore.

Thus far, Matthew has recorded very public evidences that Jesus is Immanuel, God with us, while at the same time acting as a human!

Jesus singled out Peter and asked, "Who do you say I am?" (Matt. 16:15). Peter answered, "You are the Messiah, the Son of the living God" (Matt. 16:16). *Christ*, or *Messiah*, thrusts into our minds the special anointed person promised frequently in the Old Testament. That is the testimony Jesus wanted us to hear, for that is the key to the kingdom of heaven. The testimony is, "On this rock I will build my church" (Matt. 16:18), a new fellowship. (In the Greek language, there is one word that means "belonging to the Lord," while a different Greek word means "assembly," used for a small group or as a category.) In the four Gospels, *church* is used only here. We await for an elaboration of the meaning. Here it is implied that the church will center upon Jesus the Christ, who is really Immanuel, God with us, the ultimate foundation.

Peter, James, and John, on a mountaintop with Jesus, observed him transfigured! They watched as Jesus talked with Moses and Elijah! A voice called out, "This is my Son, whom I love; with him I am well pleased. Listen to him!" (Matt. 17:5). A second imprimatur! Jesus instructed them not to tell of this until after he had been raised from the dead.

You must be like a child to enter heaven. Anyone hindering a child by one's lifestyle is subject to the eternal fire of hell.

Gather two or three people together, ask in prayer, and it will be done by his Father in heaven. That is loving provision.

Matthew now records Jesus's four declarations of his death and rising again to life:

- "He must be killed and on the third day be raised to life." (Matt. 16:21)
- "Don't tell anyone what you have seen, until the Son of Man has been raised from the dead," Jesus said after the transfiguration. (Matt. 17:9)
- "The Son of Man is going to be delivered into the hands of men. They will kill him, and on the third day he will be raised to life." (Matt. 17:22–23)

- "The Son of Man will be delivered over to the chief priests and the teachers of the law. They will condemn him to death and will hand him over to the Gentiles to be mocked and flogged and crucified. On the third day he will be raised to life!" (Matt. 20:18–19)

How could they possibly believe that?

In diverse circumstances, time and again, unmerited love was replaced by unfailing love!

Jesus entered Jerusalem on a donkey, a beast of burden, according to the revelation given to Zechariah (Zech. 9:9). Crowds leading and following shouted, "'Hosanna to the Son of David! Blessed is he who comes in the name of the Lord! Hosanna in the highest!'" (Matt. 21:9). (*Hosanna*, meaning "save now," is used as praise.)

For several days Jesus healed, taught, and warned of false teachings. Regarding the resurrection, Jesus said, "Have you not read what God said to you, 'I am the God of Abraham, the God of Isaac, and the God of Jacob'? He is not the God of the dead but of the living" (Matt. 22:31–32). When Jesus speaks of rising from the dead, he means rising from among the dead ones, the existing ones who have been separated from earth-life.

The greatest commandment is, "'Love the Lord your God with all your heart and with all your soul and with all your mind.' . . . The second is like it: 'Love your neighbor as yourself.' All the Law and the Prophets hang on these two commandments" (Matt. 22:37–40).

Jesus declared, "This gospel [good news] of the kingdom will be preached in the whole world as a testimony to all nations, and then the end will come" (Matt. 24:14). That is the breadth of God's love. The earth will change. "Great distress, unequaled from the beginning of the world until now . . . See, I have told you ahead of time" (Matt. 24:21–25). "Then will appear the sign of the Son of Man in heaven. And then all the peoples of earth will mourn when they see the Son of Man coming on the clouds of heaven, with power and great glory. And he will send his angels with a loud trumpet call, and they will gather his elect from the four winds, from one end of the heavens to the other" (Matt. 24:30–31). "But about that day or hour no one knows, not even the angels in heaven, nor the Son, but only the Father" (Matt. 24:36). Two people will be working together when suddenly one will be gone. "Therefore keep watch, because you do not know on what day your Lord will come" (Matt. 24:42). It is now two thousand years later!

When the Son of Man comes, there will be a separation, illustrated by Jesus as a shepherd placing the sheep on his right and the goats on his left. Inviting those on his right, the King (context, the Son of Man) will say, "Come, you who are blessed by my Father; take your inheritance, the kingdom prepared for you since the creation of the world" (Matt. 25:34). The King will say to the group on the left, "Depart from me, you who are cursed, into the eternal fire prepared for the devil and his angels" (Matt. 25:41). "Then they will go away to eternal punishment, but the righteous to eternal life" (Matt. 25:46). Both endings are for eternity!

In simple words, the separation will be between those who by free will accepted the Lord's sovereignty and those who by free will did not. The latter will be granted their wish: separation—eternal separation. That moment was hinted at when the title *God* changed to *Lord God* (Genesis 2:4), one who is entitled to declare, "You live" or "You die."

Late in the week, Jesus ate the Passover meal with the disciples. He announced that one of them, Judas, would betray him, and Jesus gave him a warning. Jesus knew that this was his last meal with his disciples before his arrest. Jesus gave thanks, broke and passed the bread, and added, "Take and eat; this is my body" (Matt. 26:26). Giving thanks and passing the cup, he said, "This is my blood of the covenant, which is poured out for many for forgiveness of sins" (Matt. 26:28). That's exactly what the name "Jesus" was to convey!

Jesus and the disciples sang a hymn and left for the garden of Gethsemane. En route, Jesus declared that Peter would disown him three times. Peter did! At the garden, Jesus stepped aside with Peter, James, and John and then went a few feet farther alone. He prayed, "My Father, if it is possible, may this cup be taken from me. Yet not as I will, but as you will" (Matt. 26:39). He prayed a second time: "My Father, if it is not possible for this cup to be taken away unless I drink it, may your will be done" (Matt. 26:42).

Opposition had been rising from religious leaders, ironically, who even desired to kill Jesus. He was arrested with Judas's help—betrayal, as Jesus had warned. Did they use a sword? No. Why weren't they afraid that Jesus would blind or kill them? Later, Judas killed himself. Jesus said to those who had come to arrest Him, "Do you think I cannot call on my Father, and he will at once put at my disposal more than twelve legions of angels? But how then would the Scriptures be fulfilled that say it must happen in this way?" (Matt. 26:53–54). Looking back after the crucifixion, we see that the word *Scriptures* was likely a reference to Isaiah chapter 53.

Jesus was taken to Pilate, who had one central question: "Are you the king of the Jews?" (Matt. 27:11). Had Pilate remembered the visit of the three foreigners? "You have said so," Jesus answered. Pilate did not react as Herod did. We suppose his scouts had reported that Jesus had often spoken of forgiveness and of peace and that he had never encouraged rebellion, gathered arms, or encouraged public demonstrations. It is likely that Pilate wished to have Jesus continue in his domain. Pilate had heard that it was the religious leaders who had been opposing Jesus, and that now they wanted Jesus dead. Addressing them, Pilate asked, "What shall I do, then, with Jesus who is called the Messiah?" (Matt. 27:22). Pilate recognized the Scriptures and politely invited them to do the same!

The people responded, "Crucify him!" That meant that they did not want him killed by sword in private, but they wanted a public crucifixion. There had not been a crime. Pilate relinquished his authority. Pilate had little *backbone*, even though he had a *wishbone*. Soldiers took time to mock and abuse Jesus as they proceeded toward crucifixion. They also crucified two other men, one on each side of Jesus. People mocked. Religious leaders mocked, even taunting him with the title of "Son of God." How sad.

God did not intervene on behalf of Jesus; however, he did provide observers with three hours of darkness, as though people should not be watching this happen, but rather should be considering the awesome purpose of the crucifixion. Jesus called loudly so that all present could hear: "My God, my God, why have you forsaken me?" (Matt. 27:46). Since Jesus had recognized God's purpose at the time of his prayer the night before, he had no fear of being forsaken. This was a teaching moment. Jesus called for all to recognize God's purpose—that he, the innocent one, was there as a substitute for each one of them so that they would not be forsaken by God. Life for life. God had done the same for Adam and Eve using an animal. Here was *the* sacrifice (offered by God) in place of animals (offered by people). Christ Jesus in his very being and behavior is the perfect and final sacrifice! That is God's ultimate unfailing love!

God saluted this event further by tearing the sacred curtain in the temple from top to bottom, by causing earthquakes, and by raising some people in tombs from death to life. After this resurrection, these resurrected ones spoke to many people! Upon seeing these things, some concluded, "Surely he was the Son of God" (Matt. 27:54). At evening, a follower of Jesus named Joseph asked Pilate for Jesus's body, and Joseph of Arimathea placed the body in his own tomb.

Soon the religious leaders recommended that Pilate secure the tomb, which he did.

The morning after the Sabbath, as Mary Magdalene and the other Mary approached the tomb, an earthquake occurred and an angel rolled aside the cover stone. The guards saw! The angel assured the women, "He is not here; he has risen, just as he said" (Matt. 28:6) They were to tell his disciples that he had risen from the dead, and they were to meet him in Galilee. Jesus briefly met the women as they hurried to tell the disciples.

The guards reported the empty tomb and were paid off to say that the disciples had stolen the body (Matt. 28:11–15).

Yes, Jesus met the eleven in Galilee, and apparently he had one subject in mind:

All authority in heaven and on earth has been given to me. Therefore go and make disciples of all nations, baptizing them in the name of the Father and of the Son and of the Holy Spirit, and teaching them to obey everything I have commanded you. And surely I will be with you always, to the very end of the age. (Matt. 28:18–20)

He would be with them! It is the same for us today! Again we see God's unfailing love. It is not exclusively for the Jews, but is for all nations and cultures! All authority has been given to him! He has the imprimatur from the Father, control over the spirit world, and power over the earth (storm, disease, our lives, and even his own life).

We respect an author who, upon opening a subject, later gives some definition and conclusion. In his opening, Matthew gained the attention of the Hebrew folk by using the name "Christ." Matthew recorded the actions of Jesus as Savior, even telling us that Jesus said he was "God with us." Jesus discarded civil kingship and began to show his style of kingdom and the desired response thereto. In the face of Jewish pride, Matthew recorded declarations that the love and provision of God are for all nations. Any matter left unclear to us is entrusted to God's continuing unfailing love. We await the destruction of Satan. We await the progress for all nations. We await the return of Christ.

Chapter 53 of Isaiah was inconceivable until we saw the crucifixion. The gift of the life of Jesus as a substitution for each one of us obliterates any merit on our part. Since it is life (inner being or soul) substitution, the list of one's sins, whether short or long or grievous, is immaterial. In deep humility, we call the day on which Jesus endured the cruelty on the cross "Good Friday."

Matthew appears to be an epilogue for all that has preceded, and has already been a prologue for whatever will follow. *Thank you, Holy Spirit, editor in chief, for your guidance.*

There are two ways to use what the editor in chief (the Holy Spirit) has given us: we can use it as a book and we can use it as a catalogue. Many believers only use the Book as a catalogue (memorizing favorite phrases). That obliterates the skill and intent of the authors and of the Holy Spirit to teach from the history, even with repetition. This history is a bundle of evidence for the validity of the sentences when reading from the Bible as a catalogue. May every believer have tears of joy and tears of weeping as the Holy Spirit hovers over them as they read the "Book" *and* read the "Catalogue."

It needs to be recognized that there has not been any definition of abuse of the people by the Roman government in the book of Matthew nor any delving into self-pity.

Now we are ready to read Mark!

FROM MARK

Mark surprises us by not giving details of the birth or youth of Jesus, but begins with John the Baptist. However, the heading already concludes that Christ (Messiah) is the Son of God, and in using *Messiah*, it likely brought reminders of the prior writings of the Old Testament.

This is the gospel—good news!

Mark recorded picturesque details Matthew had not, and Mark left out some conversations that Matthew recorded. The significance is that the Messiah will baptize "with the Holy Spirit" (Mark 1:8). Upon the baptism of Jesus, a voice from heaven adds, "You are my Son, whom I love; with you I am well pleased" (Mark 1:11).

With one short sentence, Mark records that Jesus was tempted by Satan.

Next, with John the Baptist already in prison, Jesus declared from Galilee in the north, "The time has come . . . The kingdom of God has come near. Repent and believe the good news!" (Mark 1:15).

Jesus met a man who had an evil spirit who called out, "What do you want with us, Jesus of Nazareth? Have you come to destroy us? I know who you are—the Holy One of God!" (Mark 1:24). That is an astounding testimony, especially since it is from an "enemy." The public was amazed at this new teaching and authority from Jesus.

Mark was not one of the twelve disciples. Many scholars believe that Mark learned while traveling with Peter. They believe he wrote while in Rome, likely having gentile readers in mind.

Jesus healed many and various diseases and drove out demons of those who came to the door. He spoke in their synagogues. He healed by speaking and touching. Even in desolate places, the crowds came. Jesus observed the faith of four men who brought a paralytic man—through the roof. Jesus told him, "Son, your sins are forgiven" (Mark 2:5). The teachers of the law accused Jesus of blasphemy. Jesus then demonstrated his realm of spiritual authority by using his physical authority and healing the man. Mark characterized the crowd's reaction as amazement a dozen times throughout his book.

Jesus ate with Levi and other tax collectors, saying, "I have not come to call the righteous, but sinners" (Mark 2:17). Often evil spirits were involved who fell before him in worship and proclaimed, "You are the Son of God" (Mark 3:11). Jesus commanded them not to identify him.

Jesus called twelve men, including Judas, to follow him. We know them as apostles.

Some religious teachers claimed Jesus was driving out demons by the power of Beelzebub. Jesus gave a short response and then said sternly, "Truly I tell you, people can be forgiven all their sins and every slander they utter, but whoever blasphemes against the Holy Spirit will never be forgiven" (Mark 3:28–29). They had accused him of having an evil spirit.

Addressing a small group, Jesus said, "Whoever does God's will is my brother and sister and mother" (Mark 3:35). Notice that there is no mention of a human father, apparently so that Jesus could reserve the use of *father* for "My Father." Maybe Joseph had died.

Mark recorded only a few of the parables that Jesus had told. Once, after testing the disciples with a storm, Jesus brought calm merely by his words. Another time a man with evil spirits called to Jesus, "What do you want with me, Jesus, Son of the Most High God? In God's name don't torture me!"

Jesus asked him, "What is your name?"

He answered, "Legion, for we are many." The demons begged not to be sent away. Jesus gave them permission to enter a herd of pigs, which panicked and drowned. The man was "in his right mind" after the demons had been cast out. The crowd apparently ignored him and begged Jesus to leave town. The man spread the incident among the nearby villages with responses of amazement (Mark 5:7–20).

A woman who had been ill for years touched Jesus's cloak and was healed. Jesus explained that it was by her faith, her trust in him. Another miracle occurred when a synagogue ruler was told that his daughter had died. Jesus gave a new concept, saying she was only asleep. His words were simply, "Get up" (Mark 5:41). She got up and was completely fine.

Mark records many miracles that Matthew had also recorded. From this point on, Mark emphasizes teaching rather than miracles. Repeating the questioning of Peter, he records the same response from Peter that was given in Matthew: "You are the Messiah" (Mark 8:29).

Mark mentions Jesus's caution to deny oneself to follow Jesus, and he applies it differently than Matthew: "If anyone is ashamed of me and my words . . . the Son of Man will be ashamed of them when he comes in his Father's glory with the holy angels" (Mark 8:38).

Following Jesus involves a careful lifestyle, even an element of servitude. Jesus told one rich young man that he needed to sell his great wealth if he wanted to follow him (Mark 10:21).

"Anyone who will not receive the kingdom of God like a little child will never enter it" (Mark 10:15). A child has a parent to guide him or her. A believer has the Father and Jesus, while he was here to guide, and now the Holy Spirit. That is loving care. At his last meal, Jesus referred to the kingdom as future. Both Matthew and Mark often refer to the kingdom.

Twice Mark records that Jesus predicted that he would be killed, but also that he would rise again.

Mark and Matthew both frequently tell of the amazement of the crowd in reaction to Jesus's teaching and miracles. Mark recorded a few references to the Old Testament.

The grand, humble entry into Jerusalem included shouting, "Blessed is the coming kingdom of our father David!" (Mark 11:10). That tells us that the Jewish people had the prophecies of a special ruler of the lineage of David in mind. On their behalf, Jesus extended the application by his clear statement, "My house [domain] will be called a house of prayer for all nations" (Mark 11:17, quoted from Isa. 56:7). Opposition from the religious leaders rose to such a pitch that they desired to kill. Despite such opposition, Jesus taught others to "Have faith in God." He told them not to doubt, but to believe. He said, "Therefore I tell you, whatever you ask for in prayer, believe that you have received it, and it will be yours . . . If you hold anything against anyone, forgive them, so that your Father in heaven may forgive you your sins" (Mark 11:22–25). That is some responsibility!

In the midst of further teaching, the subject of resurrection arose: "When the dead rise, they will neither marry nor be given in marriage; they will be like the angels in heaven . . . Have you not read in the Book of Moses, in the account of the burning bush, how God said to him, 'I am the God of Abraham, the God of Isaac, and the God of Jacob.' He is not the God of the dead, but of the living" (Mark 12:25–27). This may be a hint that the future includes a new kingdom.

The future events described next, in Mark 13, seem quite undesirable:

Many will come in my name, claiming, "I am he," and will deceive many . . . Nation will rise against nation . . . The gospel must first be preached to all nations [cultures] . . . Brother will betray brother to death, and a father his child. Children will rebel against their parents and have them put to death . . . Let those who are in Judea flee to the mountains . . . Pray that this will not take place in winter, because those will be days of distress unequaled from the beginning . . . False messiahs and false prophets will appear and perform signs and wonders to deceive, if possible, even the elect. So be on your guard . . . But in those days, following that distress, "the sun will be darkened, and the moon will not give its light; the stars will fall from the sky, and the heavenly bodies will be shaken."

Even this is part of God's unfailing love!

At that future time, "people will see the Son of Man coming in clouds with great power and glory. And he will send his angels and gather his elect from the four winds, from the ends of the earth . . . Truly, I tell you, this generation [race] will certainly not pass away until all these things have happened. Heaven and earth will pass away, but my words will never pass away" (Mark 13:26–31). When will this happen? "No one knows, not even the angels in heaven, nor the Son, but only the Father. Be on guard! Be alert! You do not know when that time will come" (Mark 13:32–33).

Mark gives the same scene as Matthew of the last meal when Jesus offered bread representing his body and the cup representing his "blood of the covenant" (Mark 14:24). Then at Gethsemane Jesus prayed, "My soul is overwhelmed with sorrow to the point of death" (Mark 14:34).

Upon the arrest of Jesus led by Judas, Jesus was taken to the high priest, where there were many accusations against him. He did not speak in response. When asked if he were the "Messiah, the Son of the Blessed One," he answered clearly, "I am." He added, "And you will see the Son of Man sitting at the right hand of the Mighty One and coming on the clouds of heaven" (Mark 14:61–62). That is the same as in Matthew. Jesus often gave a broader answer than the question required.

Again the record is the same here in Mark as it was in Matthew. Pilate asked if Jesus were king of the Jews, and Jesus affirmed that he was. As Pilate asked what was to be done to the king of the Jews, the loud response was "Crucify him!" Pilate released Barabbas. Pilate kept the matter in their face with the notice on the cross, "THE KING OF THE JEWS" (Mark 15:26).

During several hours of darkness, Jesus called loudly, "My God, my God, why have you forsaken me?" (Mark 15:34). Mark notes that the next loud call by Jesus was as he breathed his last.

Both Matthew and Mark indicated that Jesus spoke further, yet both only recorded this one call. Remember that two testimonies are validation, and both writers here have intentionally given only one and the same expression! Reader, we have read two of four Gospels. We have read half of the Gospel pages. The Holy Spirit has given us one expression twice. This must be significant! In other words, any other arrangement of Jesus's seven last words, or sayings, on the cross, is insignificant in comparison. The Holy Spirit presents this to be first for the reader of today!

For a moment, Jesus felt a sense of the loss of God's sovereignty much, much more so than Adam felt. Jesus knew by his prayer the night before that whatever would happen would be for God's purpose. This momentary demonstration was to draw a public confession: "I am the one—not Jesus—who deserves to be forsaken by God!" God still demonstrates unfailing love! You and I are the unlovable. The Father, who does not change, was still pleased with his Son. This was the Father providing his only Son, not another temporary animal!

A king did not die for you. *The King* died for you!

When Mary and the other Mary went to the tomb, they found it empty. A "man" assured them that "He has risen!" (Mark 16:6). They left bewildered.

Language scholars have some reason to believe that the sentences following this were not in the original text. Your Bible likely has a footnote to that effect.

FROM LUKE

Luke acknowledges previous writings, evidently the writings we know as the Old Testament. He had carefully investigated (apparently interviewed people) the life and teachings of Jesus in order to affirm what Theophilus had already been taught. Apparently Theophilus was a Christian of civil rank.

At length and in detail, Luke recorded a promise of a miraculous birth to aged parents, and the purpose of that son, John. John's purpose was to prepare people for the Lord.

At great length and in much detail, Luke recorded Jesus's birth. God sent an angel to Mary, a woman of Nazareth, announcing conception by the Holy Spirit rather than by man. When the baby was born, Mary was to name him Jesus, and he would be called the Son of the Most High and the Son of God. He would rule on the throne of David forever. God would do the impossible again, just as he had already done by allowing Elizabeth to conceive in her old age. Mary hurried to visit Elizabeth. Elizabeth's fetus responded, and Elizabeth exclaimed blessings on Mary for believing. After staying briefly and composing an extensive song of praise, Mary returned home. (This is only recorded in Luke.)

Stop! How was Luke able to interview Mary and get personal information from the wife of a stranger? He was a doctor. Matthew and Mark were not. John wrote years later.

Luke recorded that several miraculous aspects were involved in the birth of John. A commission was given: "Go on before the Lord to prepare the way for him, to give his people the knowledge of salvation through the forgiveness of their sins, because of the tender mercy of our God" (Luke 1:76–78). God's love includes giving us knowledge and understanding.

God used a civil census to cause Mary and Joseph to visit Bethlehem. Without fanfare, the child was born in a manger. With the usual animals present, there was warmth and no rowdiness. (This is only found in Luke.)

An angel appeared to ordinary shepherds nearby and announced, "Today in the town of David a Savior has been born to you; he is the Messiah, the Lord." The angel told them that they would find the baby "wrapped in cloths and lying in a manger" (Luke 2:11–12). A multitude of heavenly hosts appeared and announced, "Glory to God in the highest heaven, and on earth peace to those on whom his favor rests" (Luke 2:14;

cf. Luke 4:19). The shepherds hurried, found the baby as foretold, and in amazement told people what they had heard and seen. Mary pondered everything in her heart. After proper circumcision and naming the baby "Jesus," Joseph and Mary went to Jerusalem to consecrate their firstborn male to the Lord.

While they were at the temple, the Holy Spirit revealed to an elderly man, Simeon, that he would see the Lord's Christ ("Messiah"). Simeon did see him, and he held the baby, praising God: "Sovereign Lord, . . . my eyes have seen your salvation, which you have prepared in the sight of all nations: a light for revelation to the Gentiles, and the glory of your people Israel" (Luke 2:26–32). Simeon continued, "This child is destined to cause the falling and rising of many in Israel, and to be a sign that will be spoken against . . . And a sword will pierce your own soul too" (Luke 2:34–35). This child is also for gentiles! God's love is for all people!

When Jesus was twelve years old, Mary and Joseph took him to the temple, according to custom, and inadvertently left him behind. He had been busy discussing with the teachers in ways that amazed them. When his parents found him in the temple courts and questioned him, Jesus responded, "Didn't you know I had to be in my Father's house?" (Luke 2:49). They did not understand. Mary treasured these matters in her heart, and Jesus grew before people and God.

John the Baptist had considerable audiences as he urged repentance and baptized many. He recommended a changed lifestyle, which included sharing and being honest. He insisted that he was preparing the way and that indeed there was good news ahead. God's love for all!

Luke recorded the baptism of Jesus and God's imprimatur voice. (This is the third record; hence it is significant.) He recorded Jesus's genealogy all the way back to Adam, the son of God. Notice that by not starting with Abraham, he appealed to all humanity.

One day in a synagogue, Jesus read from a Scripture scroll, "The Spirit of the Lord is on me, because he has anointed me to proclaim good news to the poor . . . to proclaim the year of the Lord's favor" (Luke 4:18–19).

He had read from Isaiah 61:1–2. Jesus declared, "Today this scripture is fulfilled in your hearing" (Luke 4:21). This was good news to folks. The people in the synagogue were furious, but Jesus walked away.

Demons called Jesus the Son of God. He commanded them to be quiet because they knew he was the Christ. It is great affirmation when your enemy gives accolades! Jesus taught and healed many, as reported before. After noting Peter's correct conviction that Jesus was the Christ, Luke proceeded with, "Truly I tell you, some who are standing here will not taste death before they see the kingdom of God" (Luke 9:27). Luke recorded references to a kingdom almost as many times as Matthew, with the emphasis on people therein rather than to a king thereof. We have responsibility in living! It has been implied that Jesus will be the future king.

Luke also gives us Jesus's parable of a Samaritan helping an injured man after others had passed by. Jesus approved of him for acting as a neighbor. Note that when Jesus asked the religious leader which man had acted like a neighbor, the religious leader did not answer, "The Samaritan," but said, "The one who had mercy on him." Jesus had contradicted society. "Go and do likewise" (Luke 10:37). (This parable is found only in Luke.)

Listen to this end of a discussion from Jesus: "But if I drive out demons by the finger of God, then the kingdom of God has come upon you" (Luke 11:20). Some aspect of the kingdom is experienced and seen now.

Hearken: "Do not be afraid, little flock, for your Father has been pleased to give you the kingdom . . . Provide . . . a treasure in heaven that will never fail . . . For where your treasure is, there your heart will be also" (Luke 12:32–34).

Referring to the kingdom of God, Jesus said, "People will come from east and west and north and south, and will take their places at the feast in the kingdom of God" (Luke 13:29). On the other hand, many will make excuses. Unselfishness is deeply involved in being a disciple. The Law and Prophets had been emphasized in the past, but now this good news has arrived: God's love invites all people!

Take a moment for the parable of the loving father. Upon the wayward, detestable, unlovable son repenting and returning home, the father "saw him and was filled with compassion for him; he ran to his son, threw his arms around him and kissed him" (Luke 15:20). Our God did this even more so, for our Father of unfailing love did not kill a fattened calf, but his Son!

Now consider Jesus's parable of a rich man and a beggar. Upon death, angels carried the beggar to Abraham's side. The rich man found himself in a place of utter torment and cried to Father Abraham, saying, "I am in agony in this fire" (Luke 16:24). The answer was that each destiny was determined, and neither person could cross over to the other. The rich man pleaded on behalf of his brothers, proposing that someone from the dead could visit his brothers and warn them. Twice Abraham succinctly said, "They have Moses and the Prophets, let them listen to them" (Luke 16:29, 31). Moses and the prophets had been long dead, so the blunt advice was to read what was already written. Period! God so loves people that what God considers important is understandable.

Ah—some clarification: "The coming of the kingdom of God is not something that can be observed . . . because the kingdom of God is in your midst" (Luke 17:20–21). The subject occurs many times in Matthew, as well as in Mark. Many people have written books about this subject.

A warning: One sentence in the Book can be taken out of context! For example: "But those enemies of mine who did not want me to be king over them—bring them here and kill them in front of me" (Luke 19:27). This sentence can be taken out of context and applied in a way not intended by God. In context, we see that this sentence is part of a whole parable of encouragement!

Having concluded this much with encouragement, Luke skips to Jesus's grand entry into Jerusalem (Luke 19:28–44). Jesus entered with the humbleness of using a donkey, a beast of burden. Undoubtedly, children had run ahead to announce that Jesus was coming. A crowd of followers gave loud praises. Jesus wept over Jerusalem for not understanding his purpose and the immense destruction sometime in the future!

Jesus taught daily and repeated a basic statement of faith. He said that the Lord is "'the God of Abraham, and the God of Isaac, and the God of Jacob.' He is not the God of the dead, but of the living, for to him all are alive" (Luke 20:37–38). Luke again gave encouragement prior to recording discouragement. There will be disasters by nature, by cultures, within families, by persecution, and even "Jerusalem will be trampled on by the Gentiles until the times of the Gentiles are fulfilled" (Luke 21:24). Also, the Son of Man will arrive in conspicuous glory. "When these things begin to take place, stand up and lift up your heads, because your redemption is drawing near" (Luke 21:28).

At the Last Supper, Luke recorded an additional thought. He recorded that this covenant was new, being established by Jesus's blood and not by the life of an animal.

When the teachers of the Law asked Jesus if he were the Christ, he broadened the subject to include that he, the Son of Man, would be seated at the right hand of the mighty God! Upon being asked again, Jesus gave a direct answer: "Correct." Their response: "Blasphemy!" Pilate declared three times that he had found no fault in Jesus. However, he ended up surrendering to the clamor.

Luke skips Jesus's words, "My God," from the cross. The first word of Jesus from the cross that Luke gives is "Father, forgive them, for they do not know what they are doing" (Luke 23:34). That is amazing after such repeated mental and physical abuse! (Many leaders today present this word as having been spoken prior to the "My God.") After suffering such extensive mental and physical abuse, could Jesus forgive? Yes—including forgiving you and me. That's love!

Next is a very beautiful moment. One of the dying men on a cross next to Jesus made a request of Jesus. He said, "Jesus, remember me when you come into your kingdom" (Luke 23:42). Give the man credit for being ashamed of his rebellious life. He must have heard Jesus teach about forgiveness and understood that Jesus alone had the right to forgive sins and that somehow Jesus had in mind a different kind of kingdom than an earthly one. Gently and without rebuke, Jesus answered, "Truly, I tell you, today you will be with me in paradise" (Luke 23:43). Surely there were tears of joy! That man on that cross died, was separated from his earth-life, and was ushered into the next life. Don't try to describe paradise. It is enough to emphasize his being with Jesus. Note that Jesus ignored the man's list of sins (behavior) and honored the attitude (inner being) of believing. And this man was a Roman citizen!

One more word of Jesus is recorded by Luke: "Father, into your hands I commit my spirit" (Luke 23:46). (All three of these words from Jesus on the cross are unique to Luke.)

Luke gives much more emphasis than the other Gospel writers to the actions of the women finding the tomb empty and having a conversation with the resurrected Jesus. People had difficulty believing their report. Peter himself wondered what he saw.

Astoundingly, Jesus appeared incognito (his body appearing humanly normal) alongside two people who were discussing the recent events, including the empty tomb. Jesus reminded them: "And beginning with Moses and all the Prophets, he explained to them what was said in all the Scriptures concerning himself" (Luke 24:27). (This is mentioned only in Luke.)

Luke closes with Jesus appearing in the midst of the disciples, showing them his hands and feet (not incognito). He ate. "Everything must be fulfilled that is written about me in the Law of Moses, the Prophets and the Psalms" (Luke 24:44). Jesus thus affirmed the Old Testament! Jesus used Scripture that we read today! Jesus continued: "This is what is written. The Messiah will suffer and rise from the dead on the third day, and repentance for the forgiveness of sins will be preached in his name to all nations, beginning at Jerusalem. You are witnesses of these things" (Luke 21:46–48). Jesus would send them, but they would need to wait for power from on high.

Soon he left them, rising up to heaven. The disciples returned to the temple praising God.

We now know that the temporary animal life sacrificial system has been replaced! Jesus the Christ is the only adequate life given for you and me. By believing that, you who are of any culture and who are in any place on earth are a gem on the ring of God's love!

You were born to be loved. In the future you will be called God's "treasured possession" (Mal. 3:17—almost the last sentence of the Old Testament).

A reader asks God,

"Me, a rebel in society, forgiven by you, Lord God?"

"Yes, you."

"Me!"

FROM JOHN

We have now read the first three Gospels in the sequence given to us. The first two, being very similar, validate the message. The third adds extra records. It is amazing that three human authors, without contradicting, but blending, form the authority for us to read the life of Jesus Christ two thousand years later. This must be the hidden guidance of the Holy Spirit!

Many scholars believe that most of the Epistles had been written a little prior to these three Gospels. During these early decades, copies had been made and were slowly circulated among villages. Try to conceive the labor involved in making copies—with no electronic help!

Apparently the Holy Spirit considered this bundle of writings to be adequate, at least for several decades. The Gospel of John was likely written toward the end of that first century. (There is much debate regarding the dating. Again, enjoy reading a separate book explaining the formation of the canon.) In God's time, the Holy Spirit as editor in chief directed John to write. Humanly speaking, John had ample opportunity to sense the use and, likely, some misuse of these new books of Scripture, along with being aware of popular Greek conceptions of life. Apparently John had been vocal or had presented short writings, for he had been banished into exile—God's loving way of protection.

After the Gospel of John, we will come to pages and pages about the responsibility of changing one's behavior. Now we are ready to read from the quill of John.

The book of John startles us. "In the beginning was the Word, and the Word was with God, and the Word was God. He was with God in the beginning" (John 1:1–2). "He came to that which was his own, but his own did not receive him. Yet to all who did receive him, to those who believed in his name, he gave the right to become children of God—children born not of natural descent, nor of human decision or a husband's will, but born of God" (John 1:11–13). "No one has ever seen God, but the one and only Son, who is himself God . . . has made him known" (John 1:18). John presents in a few words that Jesus was God. He also presents the purpose for the earthly visit—that those who believe are considered by God to be his children! That's love!

Let's add John's stated purpose for writing: "Jesus performed many other signs in the presence of his disciples, which are not recorded in this book. But these are written that you may believe that Jesus is the Messiah, the Son of God, and that by believing you may have life in his name" (John 20:30–31). Apparently the Holy Spirit helped him to be succinct. "Jesus did many other things as well. If every one of them were written down, I suppose that even the whole world would not have room for the books that would be written" (John 21:25). That is likely an exaggeration for emphasis. Let's thank God that the Book is as small as it is.

Believe and *sent* are both used often in John. *Believe* (and its forms) occurs twice as many times in John as it does in Matthew, Mark, and Luke combined. *Sent* (by God) occurs about the same number of times in John as it does in Matthew, Mark, and Luke combined.

Nicodemus, a Jewish ruler, visited Jesus at night and started a conversation. Jesus, knowing his heart, replied pointedly that a person will see and enter the kingdom of God only by being born again. The Spirit of God is the means of such a spiritual change. That change is as though you had a new beginning without the self-as-god inner being of the present moment. The issue is one's inner self and not a list of behavioral sins.

Jesus said to Nicodemus, "I have spoken to you of earthly things and you do not believe; how then will you believe if I speak of heavenly things? No one has ever gone into heaven except the one who came from heaven—the Son of Man . . . Everyone who believes in him may have eternal life in him. For God so loved the world that he gave his one and only Son, that whoever believes in him shall not perish but have eternal life" (John 3:12–16). That is our goal: eternal life! The Father cherishes that goal for you as paid for by Christ Jesus. Your responsibility, as explained in John 3, is to believe!

John the Baptist heralded Jesus: "For the one whom God has sent speaks the words of God, for God gives the Spirit without limit" (John 3:34). Several paragraphs later (in John 5), John records Jesus's emphasis: "Very truly I tell you, whoever hears my word and believes him who sent me has eternal life and will not be judged but has crossed over from death to life" (John 5:24). "I seek not to please myself but him who sent me . . . For the works that the Father has given me to finish—the very works that I am doing—testify that the Father has sent me. And the Father who sent me has himself testified concerning me . . . You do not believe the one he sent" (John 5:30, 36–38).

Somehow, Jesus was both God and human at the same time. You see, God asks and expects us to believe—not to explain. "I and the Father are one" (John 10:30). No other book can present a leader with that level of authority. None. "I have come that they may have life, and have it to the full" (John 10:10).

An ultimate pronouncement came from the lips of Jesus while he was praying: "Father, I want those you have given me to be with me where I am, and to see my glory, the glory you have given me because you loved me before the creation of the world" (John 17:24). Only Jesus can extend that invitation! You are on the unending ring of the unfailing love of God!

Ezekiel alerted us: "For I take no pleasure in the death of anyone, declares the Sovereign Lord. Repent and live!" (Ezek. 18:32). Now back to John and the words of Jesus: "I told you that you would die in your sins; if you do not believe that I am he, you will indeed die in your sins" (John 8:24). "If I had not come and spoken to them, they would not be guilty of sin; but now they have no excuse for their sin" (John 15:22).

Please don't ever claim that you cannot understand the Book. Yes, there is some mystery, but much is very clear.

The following expressions are found only in John's Gospel. John the Baptist introduced Jesus to a crowd by saying, "Look, the Lamb of God, who takes away the sin of the world! . . . I testify that this is God's Chosen One" (John 1:29, 34). This reminds us of the one "lamb" God provided for Adam and Eve.

John recorded the nighttime visit of Nicodemus with Jesus and the urgent response from Jesus that Nicodemus needed a drastic change—to be born again. There are several comparisons introduced by "I am," such as "I am the bread of life" (John 6:35). How? Jesus is the bread of God who came down from heaven to give life to the world. Each expression centers on the person and purpose of Jesus. John also recorded Jesus raising Lazarus from the dead to restored earth-life by means of his voice: "Lazarus, come out!" (John 11:43). A dead man heard!

Then Jesus gave what could be thought of as a summary of the above: "As the Father has loved me, so have I loved you. Now remain in my love. If you keep my commands, you will remain in my love, just as I have kept my Father's commands and remain in his love . . . Greater love has no one than this: to lay down one's life for one's friends" (John 15:9–10, 13). Jesus did! Just wait.

For a moment we will pull two expressions together, starting with the familiar: "Whoever believes in him shall not perish but have eternal life" (John 3:16), and "I am the way and the truth and the life. No one comes to the Father except through me" (John 14:6). God has one plan lavished upon us by love. This concept has been absolutely exclusive, beginning with page one of the Book. God demonstrated his pleasure in giving the life of a lamb, temporarily, for the world of that day. God gave with finality the life of his only Son—for the world of any day!

You were born, whether you are aware of it or not, in God's love! Do you accept God's love?

Ever since we read "us" and "our" on page one of the Book, we have been hoping to learn more about the complexity of God. Now John helps. "I will ask the Father, and he will give you another advocate to help you and be with you forever—the Spirit of truth" (John 14:16–17). "All this I have spoken while still with you. But the Advocate, the Holy Spirit, whom the Father will send in my name, will teach you all things" (John 14:25–26). "When the Advocate comes, whom I will send to you from the Father . . . he will testify about me" (John 15:26). He will convict the world. "When he, the Spirit of truth, comes, he will guide you into all the truth" (John 16:13). Jesus had said, "The Father is in me, and I in the Father" (John 10:38).

We have read of the Father and of the Son. In the pages ahead, we will learn of the Holy Spirit and his very personal relationship with people. The Holy Spirit has been given enough explanation for now.

John did not need to repeat the miracles and parables told by Matthew, Mark, and Luke. Instead, he added confirmations to be grasped.

The last week of Jesus's life is given in the book of John, with similarities to and differences from the other three Gospels. One major difference is that John included three words that Jesus uttered from the cross that were not previously recorded and that were not spoken in a loud voice. The crowd may have decreased by then. Jesus saw his mother and John, the disciple he particularly loved, and he addressed each, who were evidently standing near. Jesus said to Mary, "Woman, here is your son." To John, he said, "Here is your mother" (John 19:26–27). Note the term *woman* rather than Mary, with no special honor indicated. Note the tender personal care as Jesus committed Mary to a particular disciple, John.

"Later, knowing that everything had now been finished, and so that Scripture would be fulfilled, Jesus said, 'I am thirsty'" (John 19:28). Here, note the humanity of Jesus. Also, "When he had received the drink, Jesus said, 'It is finished'" (John 19:30). The Greek word for *finished* is given with emphasis. Note that John had recorded Jesus's intent twice (John 4:34 and 5:36). The death was public so that the world would learn of it.

Yes, the tomb was found empty, the women's visit was described a little differently, and the report of Jesus's resurrection was not at first believed. Jesus appeared to ten of the disciples. Thomas lamented that he had missed that meeting. A week later Jesus appeared to the eleven disciples. Jesus urged Thomas to touch his bodily wounds. Thomas's response was, "My Lord and my God" (John 20:28).

A third appearance from Jesus after his resurrection was at the Sea of Galilee, where he miraculously fed the disciples. Jesus personally gave Peter a hint into his future manner of death, and he also instructed Peter thrice: "Feed my lambs," "Take care of my sheep," and "Feed my sheep" (John 21:15–17).

Another note of significance is that one-third of each of the four Gospels covers about one week in the life of Jesus—the death and resurrection week. All of this shows over and over again the unfailing love of God by means of the horrible-glorious demonstration in Jesus.

John, whom Jesus loved (John 21:20), recorded *love* many more times than Matthew, Mark, and Luke. Jesus frequently urged a response: *Believe*.

Right now we need a homily using *voluntary*, *vicarious*, and *victorious*:

Voluntary: Jesus allowed this to happen, whereas he could have caused blindness among the crowd and walked away.

Vicarious: All of this is directly in our face that Jesus was a substitute, a ransom, and an atonement for each one who would believe his purpose.

Victorious: Jesus was victor over humans and over death itself. He "finished" the Father's intentions.

We still don't find Satan destroyed, but "The prince of this world now stands condemned" (John 16:11). We have an introduction to the Holy Spirit, and a new subject, the church, has been broached.

Anyone today can call Jesus "Savior"!

FROM ACTS OF THE APOSTLES

Acts (the Acts of the Apostles), written by Luke, continues Luke's Gospel by recording that Jesus appeared with the apostles for forty days (Acts 1:3). The apostle Paul records that the group was more than five hundred people (1 Cor. 15:6). Jesus's topic was the kingdom of God. Wait, for you "will receive power when the Holy Spirit comes on you; and you will be my witnesses in Jerusalem, and in all Judea and Samaria, and to the ends of the earth" (Acts 1:8). That's the extent of God's love! That is much the same as Matthew recording Jesus telling his disciples to "make disciples of all nations" (Matt. 28:19). Upon Jesus's rising out of sight, two "men" said, "This same Jesus, who has been taken from you into heaven, will come back in the same way you have seen him go into heaven" (Acts 1:11). Yes, Jesus had said he would return among clouds (Mark 13:26).

At the usual time of Pentecost, the apostles (now numbering twelve again) were startled by a strange wind and flames of fire. Even more strange, the Holy Spirit caused them to speak in other languages. Those in the crowd from many countries heard the apostles speaking in their respective languages "declaring the wonders of God in our own tongues" (Acts 2:11). Peter addressed the crowd by quoting from Joel (Joel 2:28–32), concluding, "And everyone who calls on the name of the Lord will be saved" (Acts 2:21). He unequivocally declared that Jesus is "both Lord and Messiah" (Acts 2:36). Peter pleaded for repentance and baptism for those of any culture. About three thousand were "added" then and continued in fellowship and breaking bread. Peter was the first spokesperson, reminding Jews that all this was in accord with the prophets of old. Repent and have the assurance that your sins have been wiped out by Jesus the Christ (Messiah). This new message is for all people of the earth!

Peter had power by the Holy Spirit and by the name of Jesus Christ of Nazareth. Assurance was given in one sentence: "Salvation is found in no one else, for there is no other name under heaven given to mankind by which we must be saved" (Acts 4:12).

Peter and John were arrested and released and continued speaking with prayer and the power of the Holy Spirit. When God's judgment fell upon a husband and wife, fear seized the church and others. Thus far, a church is a fellowship of believers.

Many were healed, even people from around Jerusalem.

As the apostles were teaching about this new life, they were jailed. When the officers came for them in prison they found no apostles. They did not know that an angel had led them out. The apostles testified, "We are witnesses of these things, and so is the Holy Spirit, whom God has given to those who obey him" (Acts 5:32). Anger arose, yet the apostles were released and continued teaching in the temple courts and from house to house. The number of disciples increased, which included some priests.

Seven men, including Stephen, were chosen to assist widows. Hostility arose, though, and Stephen answered their opposition with a lengthy review. The members of the Sanhedrin were furious, and Stephen "saw the glory of God, and Jesus standing at the right hand of God." Stephen then said, "I see heaven open and the Son of Man standing at the right hand of God" (Acts 7:55–56). As Stephen was being stoned, he asked the Lord Jesus to forgive his murderers. Stephen's love was imitating God's love.

One man, Saul, watched with approval. A rather unified antagonism arose, and the Christians who had been assembling at the temple were scattered miles around. Saul took the lead by putting some men and women in jail.

Even in these new places where the Christians were scattered, people told of their faith. Philip, one of the apostles, performed miracles and told the good news. Men and women responded and were baptized. Peter and John joined in Samaria (in the north) and preached.

The Spirit directed Philip westward to Gaza (on the north-south trade route) and guided him to meet an official from Ethiopia. This Ethiopian official was reading from Isaiah 53:7–8 when Philip arrived, and Philip asked him if he understood what he was reading. Philip quickly led him from Isaiah to Jesus and even baptized him. The Spirit then took Philip to other villages.

Regarding Saul, a light and a voice stopped him, blinding him. The voice of Jesus announced that he would be told what to do. In town, the Lord was directing Ananias to prepare to meet Saul. Ananias was frightened. However, Ananias placed his hands on Saul and declared that this was God's arranging. Saul received his sight, was baptized, and was introduced to leaders in Jerusalem.

The church was forced to scatter into Judea, Galilee, and Samaria and had peace there.

One day Peter had a strange vision that illustrated that the message of the gospel was for all people—just in time for him to meet Cornelius, a gentile. Peter reviewed with Cornelius and his household the life and purpose of Jesus, especially his rising from the dead, along with referencing the prophets. Even some Greeks came to believe.

Church folk from Jerusalem reviewed this new breadth of cultures: the Ethiopian of Africa, Saul at the edge of Asia, and Cornelius of Europe. They concluded, "So then, even to Gentiles God has granted repentance that leads to life" (Acts 11:18). Barnabas and Saul spent a year with the church fellowship in Antioch. The title of *Christian* began to be used there.

The atmosphere was changing with James being killed and Peter imprisoned. God had something different in mind. An angel awakened Peter, released his bonds, and led him completely outside. Peter went and knocked on the door of a house where Christians had met to pray, but they were slow to believe it was Peter who was at the door.

The church that gathered in Antioch received the Holy Spirit's directive to send Paul on a journey. Within a few years, Paul had gone on three journeys, including into what is now west Turkey and even into Greece. The message always centered upon Jesus. "Through him everyone who believes is set free from every sin, a justification you were not able to obtain under the law of Moses" (Acts 13:39). This was reaching gentiles.

Once when Paul and Silas were in prison, God released them and his jail mates by an earthquake. Paul and friends had been worshiping. Paul used the opportunity to announce, "Believe in the Lord Jesus, and you will be saved—you and your household" (Acts 16:31). He taught the jail keeper and his family, and they were even baptized.

Many Greek men and women became believers, along with some people in the synagogues. One of Paul's themes was "proving from the Scriptures that Jesus was the Messiah" (Acts 18:28). In a little more than two years, all the Jews and Greeks in the villages he visited had heard the message.

Paul was warned not to return to Jerusalem, but he did so. He was imprisoned, yet had the opportunity to explain the message to governors. The Lord told Paul, "Take courage! As you have testified about me in Jerusalem, so you must also testify in Rome" (Acts 23:11). God protected Paul several times en route to Rome, even from shipwreck.

There again, Paul used the opportunity to preach during his house arrest, which lasted at least two years!

By means of human circumstances, God lovingly arranged to have the message go to "the ends of the earth"—to many cultures touching three continents! Our Lord so loved that he assisted these first leaders—Peter, John, Philip, Paul, and several others—as they spread the message. "I have made you a light for the Gentiles, that you may bring salvation to the ends of the earth" (Acts 13:47).

ROMANS TO JUDE

FROM ROMANS

*R*OMANS WAS WRITTEN BY PAUL (SAUL), who can be partially described as a man of letters and speech, of judgment and tenderness, of logic and intensity, of broad thought and details, and for the purpose of this introduction, a man whom God yanked out of one lifestyle and placed into an absolutely new one.

Neither Paul nor Peter had yet arrived at Rome, yet Paul had compassion for a cluster of believers already there. Some believers fresh from the Pentecost revival may have started it. Paul's passion is evident in each of the writings attributed to him—how believers are living and how they should be living.

Paul's heart was to be a servant for Christ Jesus. He was soon recognized by the leadership in Jerusalem. The message is God's good news. "The gospel he promised beforehand through his prophets in the Holy Scriptures regarding his Son, who as to his earthly life was a descendant of David, and who through the Spirit of holiness was appointed the Son of God in power by his resurrection from the dead: Jesus Christ our Lord" (Rom. 1:2–4).

Paul had been praying and longed to visit the Christians at Rome.

The absolute core of the good news is "a righteousness [from God] that is by faith from first to last, just as it is written: 'the righteous will live by faith'" (Rom. 1:17; cf. Hab. 2:4). God's plan has been clear: "For since the creation of the world God's invisible qualities—his eternal power and divine nature—have been clearly seen, being understood from what has been made, so that people are without excuse" (Rom. 1:20). Those who don't want God will be allowed to have their way (free will) toward all kinds of wickedness, and hence will deserve death. God does not favor Jew nor gentile regarding judgment. Those who follow some other code of laws will also be judged. Gentiles *and* Jews are sinners: "There is no difference between Jew and Gentile, for all have sinned and fall short of the glory of God" (Rom. 3:22–23). All people need the righteousness that God provides:

> All are justified freely by his grace through the redemption that came by Christ Jesus. God presented Christ as a sacrifice of atonement, through the shedding of his blood—to be received by faith. He did this to demonstrate his righteousness, because in his forbearance he had left the sins committed beforehand unpunished . . . so as to be just and the one who justifies those who have faith in Jesus. (Rom. 3:24–26)

The atonement by Jesus was, is, and always will be effective, regardless of time. Abraham was an example of faith in God, even though he did not know Jesus Christ. Righteousness is credited because of one's faith—trust in God's provision.

The result: "Therefore, since we have been justified through faith, we have peace with God through our Lord Jesus Christ" (Rom. 5:1). "God demonstrates his own love for us in this: While we were still sinners, Christ died for us" (Rom. 5:8). God's love is never matched. We rejoice in this reconciliation! This is the recovery of our problem that was started by Adam. We now have confidence that the goal of eternal life is attainable. Laws only defined the problem.

Baptism, symbolizing death, is our dying to the effect of sin and, by the resurrection of Christ, gaining the assurance of our resurrection we will live with him because he loves us! All of this, then, includes our response (responsibility) to offer ourselves daily as though slaves to please God—slaves to God. The benefit, the result, is eternal life· "For the wages of sin is death, but the gift of God is eternal life in Christ Jesus our Lord" (Rom. 6:23). "We serve in the new way of the Spirit, and not in the old way of the written code" (Rom. 7:6).

Our hope for the future is not based upon wishful thinking, but upon the evidences that God has thrust before us.

Paul is realistic, confessing his own struggle in Romans 7:15–20! Put your name there also. Laws are powerless; the Spirit is our help. The encouragement is grand. "The Spirit himself testifies with our spirit that we are God's children. Now if we are children, then we are heirs—heirs of God and co-heirs with Christ" (Rom. 8:16–17). Suffering is included. "We do not know what we ought to pray for, but the Spirit himself intercedes for us through wordless groans . . . The Spirit intercedes for God's people in accordance with the will of God" (Rom. 8:26–27).

Reader, at this point please stop reading this book, and in your Bible at home, preferably while alone, slowly read Romans 8:28–39. Admittedly, this was encouragement for those enduring persecution at that time. The same love of God applies to you today in whatever adversity you may be in now or in whatever you anticipate for tomorrow. Besides you and me, there are millions of people who face death the next day.

For now, here is Romans 8:37–39:

No, in all these things we are more than conquerors through him who loved us. For I am convinced that neither death nor life, neither angels nor demons, neither the present nor the future, nor any powers, neither height nor depth, nor anything else in all creation, will be able to separate us from the love of God that is in Christ Jesus our Lord.

God loves us. God's love is unfailing. God loves you!

No one can condemn us. "Christ Jesus who died—more than that, who was raised to life—is at the right hand of God and is also interceding for us" (Rom. 8:34).

Paul gives illustrations from long ago, and he also provides several references. The requirement is one's inner heart, not one's conduct. "Christ is the culmination of the law so that there may be righteousness for everyone who believes" of any culture (Rom. 10:4). "For it is with your heart that you believe and are justified" (Rom. 10:10). Behavior is a responsibility, not a legal matter.

"Therefore, I urge you, brothers and sisters, in view of God's mercy, to offer your bodies as a living sacrifice, holy and pleasing to God—this is your true and proper worship" (Rom. 12:1). This is not just for Sundays. This includes loving people, even submitting to authorities.

"Let no debt remain outstanding, except the continuing debt to love one another" (Rom. 13:8). "If we live, we live for the Lord; and if we die, we die for the Lord. So, whether we live or die, we belong to the Lord" (Rom. 14:8). "For everything that was written in the past was written to teach us, so that through the endurance taught in the Scriptures and the encouragement they provide we might have hope [confidence]" (Rom. 15:4). "May the God of hope fill you with all joy and peace as you trust in him, so that you may overflow with hope by the power of the Holy Spirit" (Rom. 15:13). "God's gifts and his call" are irreversible (Rom. 11:29).

May all this good news be translated into other languages so as to be clearly understood for people of all nations to believe and obey. "To the only wise God be glory forever through Jesus Christ! Amen" (Rom. 16:27).

Notice Paul's encouragements.

YOUR CHRISTIAN TITLES AND ATTITUDES

1:7	Loved by God, saint
1:7	Receiver of grace and peace
3:20	Declared righteous
3:24	Justified before God (also Rom. 5:1, 9)
3:23	Redeemed
5:1–2	Peace with God, access to God's grace
5:2	Hope (confidence) (many references)
5:5	Received the Holy Spirit
5:9	Saved from God's wrath
5:11	Reconciled
5:21	Have eternal life
6:4	New life
6:11	Dead to sin, alive to God
6:18	Slave to righteousness
6:22	Slave to God
6:23	Gift of eternal life
7:4	Bearer of fruit
8:1	Not condemned
8:6	Life and peace
8:11	Spirit living in you
8:15	Received sonship
8:27	Spirit intercedes
8:30–33	Predestined, called, justified, glorified
8:34	Christ Jesus interceding
8:37	Conqueror
9:16	God's mercy
9:26	Child of the living God
10:3	Righteousness from God
10:13	Saved
12:1	Living sacrifice

12:2	Transformed, renewed
13:8	Debtor to love
14:8	Belong to the Lord
14:9	Christ, Lord of life
15:9	Glorify God
15:9–13	Sing, rejoice, praise, hope, joy, peace
15:14	Competent
15:16	Acceptable to God, sanctified by the Holy Spirit

Remember that God made us as the creatures he can love, and he expects love in return. Remember that Adam and Eve chose self as ruler and god, and this new inner being is hereditary. Remember that God provided the means of reconciliation—first an animal and then his Son. That means there is no earning or merit on our part. The reconciliation is free. That part is done, complete, finished! Our response should be, "How am I to please God in my attitudes and conduct?" You and I will need help. The Holy Spirit is our helper. The next one hundred pages in your Bible (to Jude) present many answers. They tell us how to live, not how to build something. The Ten Commandments are not repeated, but are "exploded" for practical daily living.

FROM FIRST CORINTHIANS

Paul claims authority in the first sentence of 1 Corinthians by stating that he writes by the will of God and wishes grace and peace upon us by the Father and Son. Paul then writes that God "will also keep you firm to the end, so that you will be blameless on the day of our Lord Jesus Christ. God is faithful, who has called you into fellowship with his Son, Jesus Christ our Lord" (1 Cor. 1:8–9). You should boast only when pleasing the Lord, giving God, not yourself, credit. We have power from God by the Holy Spirit. We are not to imitate another leader, for God has given each of us a task. "Don't you know that you yourselves are God's temple and that God's Spirit dwells in your midst?" (1 Cor. 3:16).

Our help to avoid immorality is the same as the power that raised the Lord from the dead. "Circumcision is nothing and uncircumcision is nothing. Keeping God's commands is what counts" (1 Cor. 7:19). "Yet for us there is but one God, the Father, from who all things came and for whom we live, and there is but one Lord, Jesus Christ, through whom all things came and through whom we live" (1 Cor. 8:6). Be careful with your freedom so that you do not offend anyone. Make yourself a slave to everyone so as to win as many as possible. We live to get a crown that will last forever. Flee idolatry. Today, what are the idols in our culture and in our lives in particular? Follow the example of Christ, remembering forgiveness expressed from the cross. Remember that the new covenant was established for us by Christ Jesus. "When we are judged in this way by the Lord, we are being disciplined so that we will not be finally condemned with the world" (1 Cor. 11:32). Love often includes discipline.

Paul is calling this group of believers at Corinth a church. He bids us to work together, likening us to the parts of the human body. God gives skills to each one as he determines. The greater gift is love, greater even than speaking in tongues. Any gift from God, especially involving love, is to be used for the purpose of building up the church as a whole. Read chapter 13—twice.

Now we come to chapter 15, the resurrection chapter! Christ has been raised from the dead (ones), and that is why we have the confidence that the last enemy to be destroyed is death (earth-death). Judicially, death has been destroyed. In earth time, that will be in the future. Because of the confidence found in the chapter, the concluding sentence begins with *therefore*: "Therefore, my dear brothers and sisters, stand firm. Let nothing move you. Always give yourselves fully to the work of the Lord, because you know that your labor in the Lord is not in vain" (1 Cor. 15:58).

FROM SECOND CORINTHIANS

Paul addressed this letter to the church and the saints of the region. He had defined church as those "loved by God and called to be his holy people" (Rom. 1:7).

"Praise be to the God and Father of our Lord Jesus Christ, the Father of compassion and the God of all comfort, who comforts us in all our troubles, so that we can comfort those in any trouble with the comfort we ourselves receive from God" (2 Cor. 1:3–4). Suffering and comfort go together.

God anointed us, "set his seal of ownership on us, and put his Spirit in our hearts as a deposit, guaranteeing what is to come" (2 Cor. 1:22). Here is an unusual challenge: "For we are to God the pleasing aroma of Christ among those who are being saved and those who are perishing" (2 Cor. 2:15). Our lives are observed by everybody. May our faces show that we "are being transformed into his image with ever-increasing glory, which comes from the Lord, who is the Spirit" (2 Cor. 3:18). We live for Him who died for us. "We are the temple of the living God" (2 Cor. 6:16). "Godly sorrow brings repentance" (2 Cor. 7:10). Paul's hope is that our faith continues to grow. Three times Paul pleaded with the Lord regarding a physical difficulty. God answered, "My grace is sufficient for you, for my power is made perfect in weakness" (2 Cor. 12:9).

"May the grace of the Lord Jesus Christ, and the love of God, and the fellowship of the Holy Spirit be with you all" (2 Cor. 13:14).

FROM GALATIANS

Paul wrote Galatians to argue vehemently with those in the church who had slid back into relying on the use of rules for living. "Clearly no one who relies on the law is justified before God, because 'the righteous will live by faith'" (Gal. 3:11; cf. Hab. 2:4). "But the fruit of the Spirit is love, joy, peace, forbearance, kindness, goodness, faithfulness, gentleness and self-control" (Gal. 5:22–23). Here is a challenge to put on your refrigerator door: at the end of each day, ask God which of these you need the most help with in your daily conduct. Here is a challenge and a confidence: "Whoever sows to please the Spirit, from the Spirit will reap eternal life. Let us not become weary in doing good" (Gal. 6:8–9). The basic principle for living is to ask God each morning for the Holy Spirit to guide us.

FROM EPHESIANS

In contrast to the book of Galatians, the book of Ephesians is very calm. Paul was in prison when he wrote this, but there is no claim of injustice and no emotion of self-pity. The scholars debate where he wrote from, but most conclude he was in Rome. He sent this letter and also Colossians and Philemon by means of Tychicus (see Eph. 6:21–22; Col. 4:7–9). We have written records of homilies from those first centuries. Some of those preachers frequently used the allegorical system. This book strives to use the basic meaning of words.

After standard greetings to the church in Ephesus, Paul quickly refers to spiritual blessings in Christ.

> For he chose us in him before the creation of the world to be holy and blameless in his sight. In love he predestined us for adoption to sonship through Jesus Christ, in accordance with his pleasure and will . . . In him we have redemption through his blood, the forgiveness of sins, in accordance with the riches of God's grace that he lavished on us . . . He made known to us the mystery of his will according to his good pleasure, which he purposed in Christ . . . to bring unity to all things in heaven and on earth under Christ (Eph. 1:4–10).

Lavishing is not stinginess!

Paul mentions hope several times and defines that emotion as being based upon the person and accomplishment of Christ. Otherwise you

believe in something else—in vain, as Paul had said (1 Cor. 15:2). Grasp
what is established "that you may know the hope to which he has called
you, the riches of his glorious inheritance in his holy people, and his
incomparably great power for us who believe. That power is the same as
the mighty strength he exerted when he raised Christ from the dead and
seated him at his right hand in the heavenly realms" (Eph. 1:18–20). This
is all by God's love and not by our personal works—it is a gift. "That you,
being rooted and established in love, may have power" (Eph. 3:17–18).
"And do not grieve the Holy Spirit of God, with whom you were sealed for
the day of redemption" (Eph. 4:30). Paul adds this precaution: "Submit to
one another out of reverence for Christ" (Eph. 5:21). The letter ends with,
"Grace to all who love our Lord Jesus Christ with an undying love" (Eph.
6:24). That close relationship is powerful and emotional!

FROM PHILIPPIANS

Philippians, like Ephesians, was written by Paul from jail. In case you
think you have a problem, joy and rejoicing are highlighted many times
in this letter. A good summary of the book would be, "Rejoice in the
Lord always. I will say it again: Rejoice!" (Phil. 4:4). (That is my favorite
daily verse.)

When you look in the mirror, instead of seeing yourself, see the person
of Christ:

Who, being in very nature God, did not consider equality with God
something to be used to his own advantage; rather, he made himself
nothing by taking the very nature of a servant, being made in human
likeness. And being found in appearance as a man, he humbled himself by becoming obedient to death—even death on a cross! Therefore
God exalted him to the highest place and gave him the name that
is above every name, that at the name of Jesus every knee should

bow, in heaven and on earth and under the earth, and every tongue acknowledge that Jesus Christ is Lord, to the glory of God the Father. (Phil. 2:6–11)

Bow in silence with tears.

"And my God will meet all your needs according to the riches of his glory in Christ Jesus" (Phil. 4:19). Remember that it was Paul, who was miserably abused, who wrote such praise! There is no record of those prior to the flood giving such praise.

FROM COLOSSIANS

Again, Paul was in prison when he wrote Colossians. Paul applied strong medicine to the spiritual anesthetizing that was happening to this new church. It appears he was attacking the misuse of Judaic thought and of local philosophical tenets. For this brief material, here is one cornerstone:

The Son is the image of the invisible God, the firstborn over all creation. For in him all things were created: things in heaven and on earth, visible and invisible, whether thrones or powers or rulers or authorities; all things have been created through him and for him. He is before all things, and in him all things hold together. And he is the head of the body, the church; he is the beginning and the firstborn from among the dead, so that in everything he might have the supremacy. For God was pleased to have all his fullness dwell in him, and through him to reconcile to himself all things, whether things on earth or things in heaven, by making peace through his blood, shed on the cross. (Col. 1:15–20)

The entire message centers around the person of Jesus.

FROM FIRST AND SECOND THESSALONIANS

Paul began his letter to the Thessalonians with praise for the work of that church in Thessalonica, for "your work produced by faith, your labor prompted by love, and your endurance inspired by hope in the Lord Jesus Christ" (1 Thess. 1:3). Luke had acknowledged that the church had resulted from Paul and Silas's visit (see Acts 17:1–5). Paul and Silas's loving and continued concern is evident: "May he strengthen your hearts so that you will be blameless and holy in the presence of our God and Father when our Lord Jesus comes with all his holy ones" (1 Thess. 3:13). Attention is needed for proper ethical and sexual conduct. Keep the future in view.

> Brothers and sisters, we do not want you to be uninformed about those who sleep in death, so that you do not grieve like the rest of mankind, who have no hope. For we believe that Jesus died and rose again, and so we believe that God will bring with Jesus those who have fallen asleep in him. According to the Lord's word, we tell you that we who are still alive, who are left until the coming of the Lord, will certainly not precede those who have fallen asleep. For the Lord himself will come down from heaven, with a loud command, with the voice of the archangel and with the trumpet call of God, and the dead in Christ will rise first. After that, we who are still alive and are left will be caught up together with them in the clouds to meet the Lord in the air. And so we will be with the Lord forever. Therefore encourage each other with these words. (1 Thess. 4:13–18)

"The one who calls you is faithful, and he will do it" (1 Thess. 5:24).

In the second epistle to the Thessalonians, Paul continues writing about the return of the Lord, telling that Jesus will exercise judgment. However, before that happens, someone prominent in lawlessness will come, even claiming to be God, seeking to deceive people. Paul provides a little comfort for the moment: "And now you know what is holding him back, so that he may be revealed at the proper time. For the secret power of lawlessness is already at work; but the one who now holds it back will continue to do so till he is taken out of the way" (2 Thess. 2:6–7). *Thank you, Holy Spirit, for hovering over us!*

In the meantime, you and I are very responsible for our daily living.

FROM FIRST AND SECOND TIMOTHY AND TITUS

Paul wrote very personal letters to Timothy and Titus. Both had been with Paul or had been sent by him on specific missions. It had become time to appoint local leadership. Qualities of lifestyle and teaching were to be recognized. There is a crown of righteousness awaiting us. Remember:

> If we died with him, we will also live with him;
>> if we endure, we will also reign with him.
> If we disown him, he will also disown us;
>> if we are faithless, he remains faithful, for he
> cannot disown himself. (2 Tim. 2:11–13)

Titus lists characteristics for leadership and summarizes the same for all believers: "Our people must learn to devote themselves to doing what is good" (Titus 3:14). The goal is godliness, to be like Jesus Christ.

FROM PHILEMON

Next is the unique note of Paul to Philemon, from person to person, regarding the awkward situation of a runaway Christian slave about to be returned to a Christian master. Paul, with great emotion, pleads one argument: to embrace love as greater than civil rule. Note that he dealt with this as one specific case without appraising all of society.

FROM HEBREWS

We come to the book of Hebrews. It is a book of superlatives—as though we need to know more than has already been revealed—yet this is the icing on the cake.

> In the past God spoke to our ancestors through the prophets at many times and in various ways, but in these last days he has spoken to us by his Son, whom he appointed heir of all things, and through whom also he made the universe. The Son is the radiance of God's glory and the exact representation of his being, sustaining all things by his powerful word. After he had provided purification for sins, he sat down at the right hand of the Majesty in heaven. So he became as much superior to the angels as the name he has inherited is superior to theirs. (Heb. 1:1–4)

During his time on earth, the Son was lower than the angels, yet everything was subject to him, and again he calls believers brothers. We look forward to a special rest time and an account of one's conduct on earth. Christ is our high priest. Christ has obtained our redemption by his blood, establishing a new covenant. He appeared, once only, to take away our sin—*once* (Heb. 9:28). When Jesus returns, he will bring final salvation to those who are waiting for him. We have confidence in what lies ahead.

Chapter 11 has an introduction: "And without faith it is impossible to please God, because anyone who comes to him must believe that he exists and that he rewards those who earnestly seek him" (Heb. 11:6). Many leaders of past centuries are named, and we rejoice. Then we are somber as we review other folk who "were still living by faith when they died. They did not receive the things promised; they only saw them and welcomed them from a distance" (Heb. 11:13). These people were tortured to death for the evidences of their faith. No self-pity is asked for. Neither group knew of the Christ who has since been described.

Accept Paul's wish as though he were speaking to you today:

> Now may the God of peace, who through the blood of the eternal covenant brought back from the dead our Lord Jesus, that great Shepherd of the sheep, equip you with everything good for doing his will, and may he work in us what is pleasing to him, through Jesus Christ, to whom be glory for ever and ever. Amen. (Heb. 13:20–21)

The author of Hebrews emphasized God's plans regarding eternity: eternal salvation, eternal judgment, eternal redemption, eternal Spirit, eternal inheritance, and eternal covenant.

FROM JAMES

James grabs you by the shirt and looks straight into your eyes. "You know that the testing of your faith produces perseverance. Let perseverance finish its work so that you may be mature and complete, not lacking anything. If any of you lacks wisdom, you should ask God, who gives generously to all without finding fault, and it will be given to you . . . You must believe and not doubt" (James 1:3–6). "Blessed is the one who perseveres under trial because, having stood the test, that person will receive the crown of life that the Lord has promised to those who love him" (James 1:12). We are to be a kind of firstfruits of all he created.

The book of James provides details of how to live as a child of God. Every sentence is a directive of daily living for you and me, not just for leaders. Our lives are on display, both our faith *and* our actions. Deeds are stressed six times in chapter two alone.

One's tongue needs God's help, for it is used for praise or for cursing. The kind of wisdom we receive "is first of all pure; then peace-loving, considerate, submissive, full of mercy and good fruit, impartial and sincere" (James 3:17). Resist the devil. Be humble. Patience in suffering will be available. Help others. "Whoever turns a sinner away from the error of their way will save them from death and cover over a multitude of sins" (James 5:20).

These are some ways that our lives can show our love for God.

FROM FIRST AND SECOND PETER

In First and Second Peter, the succinct opening paragraph, after the introduction, presents an epilogue for the entire New Testament. That paragraph ends with, "For you are receiving the end result of your faith, the salvation of your souls" (1 Peter 1:9). It is my favorite paragraph in the entire Book!

Suffering is a subject in these books—not for pity, but on how to handle it. The lifestyle of one spouse is intended to help the other. Our faith can be seen in one sentence: "For Christ also suffered once for sins, the righteous for the unrighteous, to bring you to God" (1 Peter 3:18). Accept this truth and the Savior!

"Cast all your anxiety on him because he cares for you" (1 Peter 5:7). More love! The devil seeks to hinder you. However, "The God of all grace, who called you to his eternal glory in Christ, after you have suffered a little while, will himself restore you and make you strong, firm and steadfast. To him be the power for ever and ever. Amen" (1 Peter 5:10–11).

God's unfailing love continues for every one of us at all times!

In Second Peter we read, "His divine power has given us everything we need for a godly life" (2 Peter 1:3). The Lord wants everyone to repent. "The day of the Lord will come like a thief. The heavens will disappear with a roar; the elements will be destroyed by fire, and the earth and everything done in it will be laid bare" (2 Peter 3:10).

FROM FIRST, SECOND, AND THIRD JOHN

These letters from John begin with a statement of validity, for John and other disciples had looked at Jesus and had touched him who had been with the Father and who had appeared to them. The purpose of these letters is to proclaim eternal life. That goal of proclaiming eternal life is stated six times just in 1 John! As a football game announcer would say, "Touchdown!"

"If we confess our sins, he is faithful and just and will forgive us our sins and purify us from all unrighteousness" (1 John 1:9). Every day is to be intentional. "Whoever claims to live in him must walk as Jesus did" (1 John 2:6).

Love is the subject numerous times in all three letters. "Dear friends, let us love one another, for love comes from God. Everyone who loves has been born of God and knows God. Whoever does not love does not know God, because God is love" (1 John 4:7–8). "God is love" is not an isolated platitude. It is bathed with evidences that began on page one of the Book!

FROM JUDE

Jude is not to be neglected. As though giving us one last warning banner, Jude succinctly teaches the right use of the Scriptures to counter certain people.

Especially note a reference to Enoch that is different from that of other canonical writers. No record is given of a vision or of an angel speaking to Jude. (Some scholars suggest this reference was copied from a non-canonical piece.) Evidently a few people throughout the millennia retained this piece of oral history (not oral tradition) to quote Enoch of the pre-flood days. Give the Holy Spirit credit for hovering over this piece: "Enoch, the seventh from Adam, prophesied about them: 'See, the Lord is coming with thousands upon thousands of his holy ones to judge everyone, and to convict all of them of all the ungodly acts'" (verses 14–15). *Thank you, Holy Spirit, for guiding leaders to include Jude in the canon.*

Throughout these latter one hundred or so pages in the Book directing believers how to live day after day, God's love is evident! God loves people whether they recognize his love or not. God's love has been unfailing, while our reciprocal love has been erratic.

Notice the progression of God's method. For the first two thousand years of human history, God did not give laws or commandments. Guidance was to be the obvious love of God. People were to love God. God gave one life (an animal), instead of the lives of Adam and Eve, to symbolize God's desire for restoration of fellowship. Next, after the flood, God gave an immense set of laws, including, once again, animal life for restoration. Again, God gave the means. That was all temporary and was not judicially adequate. Finally, the adequate life of Christ (Messiah of the old prophecies) Jesus (Immanuel, God with us) was given once. For our current age, after Christ Jesus, no set of laws or commands per se has been given. The basic command to love God was repeated several times. However, the Ten Commandments don't need to be repeated, for instead they have been "exploded" and have fallen on all these recent pages! The one basic guidance of love continues. Notice now the similarity of our current age to the pre-flood age!

Remember the application that has been given many times—that this whole message was and is for all nations/cultures. Here are two quick reflections:

1. Jesus gave the base for this explosion: "'Love the Lord your God with all your heart and with all your soul and with all your mind.' This is the first and greatest commandment. And the second is like it: 'Love your neighbor as yourself.' All the Law and the Prophets hang on these two commandments" (Matt. 22:37–40). This is applicable within any civil rule in the world!

2. The apostle Paul gave his "nutshell": "The fruit of the Spirit is love, joy, peace, forbearance, kindness, goodness, faithfulness, gentleness and self-control. Against such things there is no law" (Gal. 5:22–23).

This, too, is applicable within any civil rule in the world! So also are the hundreds of "how to live" items found in these recent pages.

Obviously, the Advocate, the Mediator, the Atonement, the Ransom—Christ Jesus—intentionally came for the whole world, whether women, men, young, or old.

"Who can fathom the Spirit of the Lord, or instruct the Lord as his counselor?" (Isa. 40:13). God is sovereign. Bow in humility with a smile in silent awe.

A reader asks God,

"Me, a man or a woman, called and loved by you, Father?"

"Yes, you."

"Me! Thank you, Lord Christ Jesus!"

REVELATION

FROM REVELATION

As though the curtain opens for an encore, we have the book of Revelation. It satisfies us when we say, "I'd like to know." We already have many assurances based upon much evidence. Oh, yes, we really would like to know how Satan will be destroyed.

On the stage, Revelation is the final act. In literature, this is called the epilogue. In the sports world, this is the overtime just before the final whistle.

Many books have been written about Revelation, so I will be brief.

The first three chapters refer to seven named, existing churches. There is praise and critique. Any church today would do well to compare itself with each of these and define needs for change. God gives time to repent (see 2 Peter 3:9).

Next comes an immense transition. John had a vision in which a voice called, "Come up here, and I will show you what must take place after this" (Rev. 4:1). John saw a throne and twenty-four other thrones, along with elders and strange creatures. They praised, "Holy, holy, holy is the Lord God Almighty, who was, and is, and is to come" (Rev. 4:8). A Lamb appearing as though it had been slain was central. Great praise ensued. "Every creature in heaven and on earth and under the earth, and on the sea, and all that is in them" gave praise (Rev. 5:13). The Lamb opened the seals. Death by sword, by famine, and by plague took place, in addition to extensive natural disasters.

Twelve thousand from each of the twelve tribes of Israel (144,000 total) met and were marked for safety. In addition, a great crowd appeared "that no one could count, from every nation, tribe, people and language, standing before the throne and before the Lamb" (Rev. 7:9). They were in white robes and gave praise. They had come out of the great tribulation. Note: they were from every culture!

A third of mankind was killed. "The rest of mankind who were not killed by these plagues still did not repent of the work of their hands; they did not stop worshiping demons, and idols" (Rev. 9:20). Gentiles "will trample on the holy city for 42 months. And I will appoint my two witnesses, and they will prophesy for 1,260 days" (Rev. 11:2–3). They will be killed and lie dead for three and a half days. The world will gloat over them until they are raised to life and to heaven. God appeals to people in most unusual ways.

A very significant war in heaven will be between Michael and his angels and the dragon and his angels. We won't see that. The great dragon (ancient serpent, devil, Satan) will lose; he will not be destroyed, but he and his angels will be hurled to earth. "He is filled with fury, because he knows that his time is short" (Rev. 12:12).

Satan puts forth two beasts with enormous power. It appears that Satan will present himself as a trinity as if to imitate God. Such power and authority are not surprising, as Jesus three times called Satan the "prince of this world" (ref. John 12:31, 14:30, and 16:11).

A distinction will take place: "Blessed are the dead who die in the Lord from now on" (Rev. 14:13). Satan's team will be destroyed by the Son of Man "harvesting" the earth (Rev. 14:16).

Angels will execute God's wrath. People who are victorious over the beast will be given harps and will sing. Others will refuse to repent. Great disasters will happen on earth. Some people will curse God.

Select earthly kings will make war against the Lamb and lose because "He is Lord of lords, and King of kings—and with him will be his called, chosen and faithful followers" (Rev. 17:14). There will be great shouting in heaven: "Hallelujah!" That will be followed by an invitation: "Blessed are those who are invited to the wedding supper of the Lamb!" The angel who was speaking then added, "These are the true words of God" (Rev. 19:9).

A rider on a white horse will be named Faithful and True and the Word of God. He will rule sternly and will bring judgment. A banner will read, "KING OF KINGS AND LORD OF LORDS" (Rev. 19:16).

Note the permissiveness and patience of God throughout these events.

Satan will be completely bound for a thousand years (Rev. 20:2). We've been waiting for such a time as this! After the thousand years, Satan will be set free for a short time! Why? Those who died for their faith will be raised to life and will reign with Christ for one thousand years. The first resurrection is for those at the beginning of the one thousand years (Rev. 20:5).

When Satan is released, he will deceive people again. Then he will be thrown into burning sulfur forever and ever (Rev. 20:7–10). That destruction by God will happen effortlessly, as by a breath (2 Thess. 2:8). Finally! *Thank you, Lord!*

The Book of Life will then be opened, and all will be raised (second resurrection) from the earth and be judged. "Anyone whose name was not found written in the book of life was thrown into the lake of fire" (Rev. 20:15). This is eternal separation!

Satan did not attack God per se, but he attacked the saints—the same way he did with Adam and Eve.

There will be a new heaven and a new earth—and a new Jerusalem as a bride prepared for her husband. "Look! God's dwelling place is now among the people, and he will dwell with them. They will be his people, and God himself will be with them and be their God. 'He will wipe every tear from their eyes. There will be no more death'" (Rev. 21:3–4). "I am the Alpha and the Omega, the Beginning and the End . . . Those who are victorious will inherit all this, and I will be their God and they will be my children" (Rev. 21:6–7). In the manner of a soccer announcer, "Goooooaaaal!" Seriously awesome! Solomon's meditation is answered: "Will God really dwell on earth?" (1 Kings 8:27; 2 Chron. 6:18). Yes!

The new Jerusalem will not have a temple, and the sun will be replaced by the Lamb as its light. Jesus had prayed for people to be with him: "Father, I want those you have given me to be with me where I am, and to see my glory, the glory you have given me because you loved me before the creation of the world" (John 17:24).

"Look, I am coming soon! My reward is with me" (Rev. 22:12). Give this testimony "for the churches" (Rev. 22:16), as listed in the first pages of the book of Revelation.

"Let the one who is thirsty come; and let the one who wishes take the free gift of the water of life" (Rev. 22:17).

A severe warning is upon anyone who tampers with this message (Rev. 22:18–19).

"Amen. Come, Lord Jesus" (Rev. 22:20).

Reader on the other side of the kitchen table: With all the current disappointments on earth, have you in desperation accepted God's unfailing love that provided Christ Jesus? He lovingly and willingly died to pay the price for your sins and to provide you with the free and sufficient gift of eternal life that will allow you to enter God's presence. Have you thanked God that you were born into such love?

The man on the cross who said to Jesus, "Remember me," did not know these revelations, but he understood Jesus's love. Likewise, a person in any culture of the world may not know, but may respond to what God has put in each soul—that there is a future and a final judgment. Such a person may join with Job and cry out that God's love would in some way provide an advocate.

EPILOGUE

DID YOU ENTER?

The Creator God has spoken! The Holy Spirit has continued to hover in unrecognizable ways in order to convict individuals, and he has used recognizable means.

He has used the consistency of many writings, the intensity of speaking, and the intention of ordinary vocabulary as evidence for the only creature capable of understanding. The Creator loves the only ones created to love!

Observe the consummation. Adam and Eve were placed in God's personal presence with the contingency of using free will. They did. The change was the heart deciding to live with self-as-god. Now a resurrected believer is given a new heart, is born again, and desires to live with God-as-God and enter the eternal life. Now no contingency is available or desirable. That means that the Lord God has declared "You live" eternally! The specter of "You die" is gone, and the correct means of address is no longer "Lord God," but "God"—or we can lovingly say "Father."

Now that you have learned about God and humanity and about God's love for each individual person, have you admitted that you approach God without merit, but actually with demerit? Have you accepted Jesus as your Savior? You don't ask, but only accept Jesus's wide-open offer. Remember, Jesus used *gate* as a figure of speech at the beginning of his ministry in his Sermon on the Mount (Matt. 7:13–14). The entry is open for your acceptance. No coercion is involved. Long ago, Jesus invited you to be with him today.

A believer, having a new heart and spirit, will enter God's personal presence, just as Adam and Eve first experienced. Then the believer will take of the gift of the water of life and a share of the tree of life!

This book is an encouragement toward the goal of reading the Bible from front to back, in a year's time, each year for the rest of your life. The familiar titles and grouping of the sixty-six books were not used in this book in order to enhance the sense of progressive unity throughout. The grouping is not rigid since there is considerable overlap of thought. The intention of God loving people is basic from the first page to the last. There is no other book like the Bible. There is no one who loves us like God! Thank God for his garment of love. The subtle influence of the Holy Spirit upon a believer cannot be measured, though it is daily lavished upon us. That reminds us that the subtle influence of Satan should be suspected—daily.

Some teachers presume they have all the details of events explained. Use the rule of caution: "I'd like to know, but maybe I don't need to know (while still here on earth)."

Perhaps you found the matter of the use of free will to be humbling, even embarrassing. Remember, using free will was how Adam and Eve started our problem. Here is a question to challenge you: Have you ever made a choice based on emotion and later rued the day?

Don't let a leader frighten you by the use of the term *election*. Jesus put the matter in our face by urging us to *believe*. John's Gospel, the epilogue of the four, recorded the use of *believe* more than fifty times. You got it? Emotion is involved, as God loves the world. Intellect is also involved. The apostle Paul succinctly stated that the fair wage for sin is death, and the wage, paid by God, is Christ Jesus himself, allowing us to avoid eternal separation and receive eternal life instead.

As you fellowship with other believers, you will find that you are part of a church, whatever the name on the front of the edifice is or no matter whose home you are in. You need the encouragement and guidance from those who study the whole Bible.

You should also now freely use the Book as a catalogue to study a word or topic, choosing topics such as Father, Son, Holy Spirit, blame, eternal, evil, forgiveness, peace, prayer, promises, sickness, and suffering. Many people have made and memorized a list of a hundred favorite sentences. Note that *verse* is a system for location. You memorize sentences. A few people are able to give time to research the Hebrew or Greek words. That, too, is thrilling.

What a thrill that you were born in God's love!

There is one God. There is one Savior. There is one eternal life.

You know more about God, though not having seen him, before you enter his eternal presence than you knew about your spouse-to-be, whom you have seen, before you entered your mutual earth-time presence!

Wishing you, a believer in Christ Jesus our Savior:

- the thrill of reading every page of your Bible in a year (then every year for the rest of your life);
- the gaining of wisdom from trained leaders;
- the habit of thanking the Holy Spirit for hovering over your life; and
- the readiness, perhaps in adversity, to separate from here and meet God.

With love and prayer,
Martin E. Ives

READING THE
ENTIRE BIBLE

Here is the apple (Prov. 7:2). Here is the honey (Rev. 10:9–10).

Read it through in a year—and every year for life!

Month 1	Genesis, Exodus
Month 2	Leviticus–Deuteronomy 17
Month 3	Deuteronomy 18–First Samuel
Month 4	Second Samuel–First Chronicles 9
Month 5	First Chronicles 10–Job 27
Month 6	Job 28–Psalms
Month 7	Proverbs–Isaiah
Month 8	Jeremiah–Ezekiel 21
Month 9	Ezekiel 22–Malachi
Month 10	Matthew, Mark, Luke
Month 11	John, Acts, Romans
Month 12	First Corinthians–Revelation

(Cut and trim to fit in your Bible.)

BOOKS BY
THIS AUTHOR ...

---

were written to urge each person to read and be thrilled by the entire Message the Holy Spirit has thrust before us ...

What's Next, Lord?	published 1997	203 pages
Jesus' Seven Words Our One Word	published 2010	75 pages
I Read the Bible, I'm Changed!	published 2013	361 pages
Alert Yield	published 2014	207 pages

and to respond in the way that the Holy Spirit guides each reader individually.

Another book, "To You. From God," is in progress.

Order Information

To order additional copies of this book, please visit
www.redemption-press.com.
Also available on Amazon.com and BarnesandNoble.com
Or by calling toll free 1-844-2REDEEM.

CPSIA information can be obtained
at www.ICGtesting.com
Printed in the USA
FSHW021834081119